D1070722

THE SULLEN ART

THE SULLEN ART

Interviews by

DAVID OSSMAN

with modern American Poets

CORINTH BOOKS

New York, 1963

DAVID OSSMAN has been associated with radio broadcasting since early 1959, when he joined the staff of WBAI in New York as an announcer. During 1960 and 1961, he also served as Production Director, consultant on literary programming, producer and book reviewer. In the winter of 1961, he joined the staff of Pacifica Radio in Los Angeles (KPFK), where he continues his activities as producer-director, actor and technical consultant in literature, drama and public affairs programming. In addition to his involvement with radio, he has had his own poetry and translations published variously. He is working on his second collection of poems, *Landscape With Mirror*.

ACKNOWLEDGMENT

All of these interviews were originally broadcast over the radio stations of the Pacifica Foundation. Three were originally published, in somewhat different forms, in *Nomad*.

COVER PHOTOGRAPH

The photograph on the cover of Robert Creeley reading to a group in San Francisco is by Ann Perkoff.

Library of Congress Catalog Card Number: 62-17664

Published by CORINTH BOOKS, Inc.
New York 11, New York
Distributed by THE CITADEL PRESS, 222 Park Avenue South,
New York 3, New York

Printed in U.S.A. by
NOBLE OFFSET PRINTERS, INC.
NEW YORK 3, N. Y.

CONTENTS

This book is for

GENE BRUCK

who gave me the chance

Introduction

Early in 1960, the idea of "The Sullen Art" as a continuing series of radio programs inquiring into the sources and future of contemporary poetry was born. I chose deliberately at that time to interview the younger poets and, inevitably, that group of poets catagorized as "new," (or sometimes and quite erroneously, as "beat"). By the end of that summer, I had recorded ten informal conversations, seven of which are printed here: Levertov, Carroll, Rothenberg, Bly, Logan, Sorrentino, and Jones, in the order of their original broadcast. The remainder were recorded later in 1960 and during 1961, and included conversations with student poets, foreign editors and traditionalists as well as with the "experimentalists."

What was "the scene" like in New York during those two years? You will find a number of references to Donald Allen's anthology *The New American Poetry 1945-1960* (Grove Press) in these interviews. That book was then both clarifying and confusing the situation of the American poetic "underground" for the general public (which had been aware only of "Howl," *On The Road* and a stir in San Francisco), but it and other anthologies and magazines *were* helping to put new poets into public consciousness. However, even the best known, (perhaps especially the best known), of these poets wrote under a flurry of inept criticism, and are still being scourged by book reviewers, editors and mass-circulation magazines for their techniques, innovations and private lives.

Despite the adverse reviews, attempts at censorship and the sudden growth of a "beatnik" craze which threatened to absorb everyone between the ages of 15 and 45, those two years were active and exciting. Things seem to have quieted down a good deal since then.

Given the uneasy attitude of the general public, I felt and still feel it necessary to point out, as Gil Sorrentino says, "that the new poets are not a bunch of illiterate, barbaric, slightly criminal types." It is my hope that these conversations on methods, influences and states of mind did help to do just that. I am sure, however, that all of these poets will live or die on the basis of their work, and that what I might have prodded them into saying here is no final defense of their position. It is merely an attempt to "set the record straight."

Nearly all the poets here know one another and name one another as influences or close friends. Such is the situation in American poetry today. The community of these new poets is small and in contact either directly or by correspondence. It bears little or no relation to the academic communities in which most other poets find themselves writing. Although a number of them do teach, or have taught college, such an institution (with the possible exception of Black Mountain) has not described the framework of their art. It would be unfortunate, however, to consider these writers members of a single "avant-garde" clique. They are too individual and independent to be taken for an organized junta in opposition to what has been variously called "The Academy" and "The Establishment." Not only have many of them been teachers, but their books, published and in preparation, total some 60 volumes. It is too bad that American poetry today appears to fall into two distinct camps. Many of these writers would readily admit the talents of others who are called their opposition.

Because some time has passed since these words were recorded, each transcript has been approved by the poet involved, generally with a minimum of editing. These are in no sense to be considered manifestoes or essays. I have tried to retain the conversational tone, informality and intimacy of the original studio interviews, though I have made my own remarks briefer and more to the precise point. Some of the questions asked may seem abrupt or even foolish. These questions, however, were deliberately phrased and invariably the responses were immediate and informative. I think that a comparison of answers to similar questions will indicate clearly the difference between poets who have been lumped together into the same "school," and will help to show in many cases how considered their art really is.

All of the 40-odd poets I have interviewed on "The Sullen Art" have been most kind and generous with their time. There are many whom I would have liked to include here, but for the lack of space. I did intend to print my conversations with Cid Corman, the influential Editor of *Origin*, and with Robert Duncan, but both asked to be left out, for personal reasons. I would like particularly to thank Jerry Rothenberg, Paul Blackburn and Denise Levertov for their help in contacting poets and for their general encouragement.

Finally, I should like to say that the title, "The Sullen Art," has no pejorative connotations. It is taken from a well-known poem by Dylan Thomas and seemed right to me for the reason that "sullen" comes from the Latin *solus*—alone. These poets, and all poets, despite their contacts with the world, are ultimately alone. One creates, after all, by one's self.

David Ossman
Burbank, California
May, 1962

Kenneth Rexroth

Rexroth is by far the oldest poet represented here, and the one with the most books to his credit. For many years he has been considered an outstanding critic and translator, and his essays on "the new poets" in such places as *The N. Y. Times Book Review, New World Writing* and *Evergreen* did much to help establish them, although his unorthodox literary position has not endeared him to "The Establishment." He lives, of course, in San Francisco.

You published several articles about new poets during 1957, at the height of interest in the San Francisco "renaissance." In one of them, you said: "I am, myself, at my advanced age, a little tired of being the spokesman for the young." How did you get to be such a spokesman?

Well, I've asked students about this—this has been going on a long time—and I really have no explanation for this rapport. They make wisecracks, they say, "because your poetry is so sexy," or something like that. It's a question I've never been able to answer satisfactorily. This has been going on all my life. I seem to associate with people of about graduate school age—about twenty to thirty. Maybe it's because a great many people kind of wear out after thirty and freeze —set in the patterns of their youth. I don't know what it is— whether it's my personality, whether it's my ideas—I have no idea what it is.

Are you still a "little tired" of being the spokesman?

I suppose the remark is ironic. No, I wouldn't say that. The great trouble, you see, is that I always have the young of about four years ago wished off on me after somebody else has discovered them. Now, I find it very interesting to talk to young people, to see the change in the climate of opinion in the colleges which has been going on. This is endlessly fascinating—you never tire of it. Incidentally, "young people" is a filthy word I think, but I don't know just how else you're going to characterize them.

Do you think you were responsible in any way for the success of the San Francisco "renaissance" poets and others like Levertov, Creeley and Olson, whom you called influential?

Well, after all, I am in a sense a part of the "establishment." I've been around an awfully long time, and I know practically everybody in literary New York of my own generation and an older generation, so that I do, to a certain extent, have the ear of publishers, editors—people like that. On the other hand, I think that's of little importance in the question of these writers, because what we are witnessing now is a widespread reaction against a period of reaction and conservativism and conformity and even persecution, and I think that these people would have made their way no matter who was there. This is what the public wants to hear today. The significant thing about Ferlinghetti, who may think he's an atypical young American, is that he's very typical. His poetry is popular because it's the way large numbers of quite ordinary educated Americans think, react to things. He's a genuinely popular poet, as of now. I think you can send a manuscript to a publisher, but sooner or later, some publisher is going to find it anyway.

Do you think the new movement in poetry spread from San Francisco or that it simply grew up of its own accord?

It's part of a world-wide pattern. In fact, it's become altogether too much of a pattern. You can sell a pair of Levi

Straus overalls on the Moscow black market to what the *Komsomolska Pravda* calls "hooligans" for $200. This type of costume, type of poetry, everything else, is spreading throughout the world. Of course, it's part of a general pattern, which, along a very wide fringe, degenerates into a vulgar craze. I think that in New York, the "establishment" is pretty well lost in the late 30's. I know all these people, and meeting old friends in the last two weeks has been kind of a shocking experience. But then, they don't have the ear anymore of much of anyone except themselves.

Do you think there's any validity in the terms "beat" or "beat generation?"

Well, there aren't very many of them—there's Jack Kerouac, Allen Ginsberg and Gregory Corso. These people are, from the point of view of the kids in the colleges today, middle-aged. They are the products of the McCarthy-Korean War period, and a period in which organized society in America was profoundly nihilistic. People talk about the "nihilistic revolt" of these writers—well, like breeds like. We lived through a period of political nihilism in high places, and it produced its opposite number, and, of course, its opposite number was very similar to itself, as is always the case in political action and reaction. I think that this is no longer very appropriate to the present situation. But, I think that there are certainly, throughout the world, large numbers of people of that age group whose attitude towards all social values, you might say to all organized, civilized life is, as the psychiatrists say, "very negativistic." And they have a case. Certainly they had a case. I think that the great danger is that this has now been turned into a commercial stereotype—it's a "hot commodity," and it is certainly used up, totally used up, for anybody who comes after. It's all right for some high school kid to hitchhike to Greenwich Village or North Beach and dress in a shirt-tail and leotards, but nothing is ever going to come of this. It's sunk now to the level of swallowing goldfish, or peewee golf.

Do you think jazz has worked as an influence on the newer writers?

Oh, writers know singularly little about music. As a matter of fact, I would say that the influence of jazz on modern poets, particularly people who, like man, dig the beat scene, like, has been most unfortunate. Nothing is more lamentable than a poetaster in a beard reciting what he considers hip potery. Writers use words, so they commonly fall for verbalisms—and in the jazz scene they fall for the jazz mystique, and as far as the musicianship of jazz is concerned, the jazz mystique is nothing but a nuisance. This doesn't mean that I think that jazz should be played before extremely solemn audiences—though to a certain extent, that's part of the mystique of jazz as a part of the entertainment business.

Isn't staying "cool" part of the order of things?

Yes, but one of the best things about Ornette Coleman or even Charlie Mingus today is that you could get up and dance to them. You could even roll and bump. The very essence of jazz is that it is an art form in which the audience participates very intimately. And I think this sense of the audience participating is a vital factor in the jazz musician's own creativity.

Is there any way of avoiding the Cult which springs up around something new and fresh?

Well, you see, we live in a commercial civilization, and we live in a civilization with a continuously rising educational standard (in spite of what educators say) and an increasingly wide reading and listening public. Now, anything in literature or the arts, or certainly anything in entertainment, very rapidly becomes a hot commodity, if it's any good. What happens, of course, is that you have crazes, many of them manufactured to sell creative expression as a commodity.

In the course of time, when this pitch has died away, when the publicity drive (it's like selling cigarettes) and the campaign has died away, the good remains—the good remains. Maybe what Madison Avenue has done is to discover that literature can be made part of the entertainment "selling technique," too.

To a degree, it's become a business insofar as readings in coffeehouses go—to the extent of their being required to have licenses . . .

There's nothing wrong with this. It can be very silly and very cheap and vulgar and commercial, but if you have a civilization in which in accepted places of entertainment you have poets reading either seriously or comically, you have something that I would say is a considerable step forward in the integration of the arts into the community. Now, it's true that poetry loses in public presentation, that is, at least it must have a public surface. That was pointed out in the case of Shakespeare—something for the pit to laugh at. But I think this is, by and large, a good thing. When the craze dies away, when the silliness dies away, there is then left behind a really rather drastic social change. Imagine if you were to prophesy, in 1925, the reading of T. S. Eliot to music in a nightclub in Kansas City or Dallas—people would have thought you were simply crazy. Sure, it represents a certain degree of vulgarization, but then so did the Greek *rhetor*—he competed with athletes, you know.

In 1957 you noted that "'Howl' is the confession of faith of the generation that's going to be running the world in 1965 and 1975, if it's still there to run." Does that have to do with these social changes following the craze?

Yes. And of course, one of the characteristics of that poem is its biblical absolutism. It has a great deal more to do with Hosea or Jeremiah than it has to do with the mystique that's attached to it. You know—people taking shots of heroin in dark corners of dismal nightclubs. The poem is a poem of a sort of irreconcilable social denunciation. Now, these chickens are already coming home to roost. All over the South today, there are men and women, some of whom might even have read "Howl," who simply have said: "Jim Crow is over, and it's over in our persons. We're not putting up with it anymore." They accept no temporization whatsoever. Note that it is not an alienated attitude—quite the opposite—it's a question of "integrate or die," and it's anything but alienated or dis-affiliated.

You say: "The problem of poetry is the problem of communication itself." What do you feel about your own poetry in terms of what it communicates?

Well, that's another thing—I've never understood why I'm a member of the avant-garde. I write more or less like Allen Tate thinks he writes—like the great Greeks and Romans and the Chinese, and so forth. I try to say, as simply as I can, the simplest and most profound experiences of my life, which I think will be of significance to others on a similar level— that is, which will touch them in significant regions of their experience. And, I suppose that my whole attitude toward poetry—toward my own poetry—is to keep always before myself an objective of clarity and depth, and hope that out of this you'll get exaltation.

You believe very much in translation, too . . .

God forbid that I should quote Ezra Pound or T. S. Eliot, but they have both pointed out that the Muse is not always at beck and call, and that the way to keep your hand in is by exercises of various kinds. What translation does for you is to provide you with poetic exercises in contact with the noblest minds—that is, if you choose to choose them. In other words, if you can't always be your own poet, you can always be, so to speak, as good an actor in somebody else's role as you can. And I think it's a good thing for a poet. It's better than sitting around and gossiping about one another's articles in the quarterlies. And the books of translations that I've done down the years have been products of a lifetime. I don't just sit down one year and dash off a hundred Greek poems and next year dash off a hundred Chinese. I've translated all my life, and I think it's a good discipline, good exercise for a poet, and I have beside me gentlemen with whom I agree on very little else. I mean Mr. Eliot and Mr. Pound.

Paul Carroll

At the time this conversation was recorded, Carroll had published three numbers of *Big Table*. The experience, he reports now, was "great and a ball," but ultimately ended in the discontinuance of the magazine early in 1961. He now is Associate Editor of *WFMT Perspective,* and produces occasional programs for that fine Chicago station. His first volume of poems is to be called *De Medici Slot Machine.* He reads Augustine "for the good of my dark Irish soul."

Why did you start Big Table? *What happened?*

Freedom. Irving Rosenthal and I were editing the *Chicago Review* and we began printing some of the San Francisco poets, who were later lovingly christened by Henry Luce as "The Beat Generation." An irresponsible columnist in Chicago—a scandal journalist—attacked the Autumn 1958 issue, and trouble started. As a result, the University of Chicago (the *Chicago Review* was University-subsidized) began to exert pressure in rather Franz Kafka ways, until finally it got to the point where they said no more financial support would be given.

Irving and I and the other editors said: "We've had it," and walked out and started *Big Table.* Irving edited the first issue (March 1959), and then got out. The Post Office banned it because of Burroughs; the whole fiasco had a marvelous surreal quality because two of the writers—Burroughs and Corso—in that issue went on to win Longview Literary Awards on the merit of their work in *Big Table* 1.

Why was the magazine called Big Table?

Jack Kerouac suggested it. We were having trouble think-ing of a title—we didn't want a square, place-name title like *Kenyon* or *Hudson*—we wanted something different. But we didn't want a chi-chi title like *Neurotica*. I wanted something very mid-western in feeling. Jack knew about this trouble and sent us a telegram saying: "Call it *Big Table*." I wrote to him later and asked him how he got that title. He said that he had a note on his writing desk: "Get a bigger table."

Does publishing a new magazine take courage or money? You seem to imply courage . . .

Well, it takes courage first, and if there's quality, you get the money. It takes money, too. I think it takes courage in the beginning, though. You stick yourself out on a limb; you're not quite sure if the stuff's good or not but you take a chance because the writers are trying.

Yet, the writers you feature are pretty well known and widely published. Don't you think the "New American Poetry" is on its way to becoming the "New American Academy?"

True. But it does take courage to send Kerouac back when he's bad, and he is bad sometimes. Ginsberg, too. I told Allen that *Big Table* was not going to be a house-organ for his Boy Scouts. When they send something good and we think it's good we print it. If it's bad, it's bad and back it goes. *Big Table* is not beat and not square: if Nixon sent me a good sonnet I'd print it.

By courage I don't mean simply fighting the Post Office—that's easy, it's like Don Quixote—but it takes courage to print writers who are not yet "in," whether the Establishment or the Hip Scene, it doesn't matter. That's how a little magazine gets and maintains life. Sometimes you may make some awful mistakes. Some of the literature you print is perishable. You can't tell at this point. I don't know where Allen Ginsberg is going to go. I have faith in his good stuff and I print it.

It's not so much courage, maybe, as a kind of commitment that there is such a thing as a new literature. I prefer to say it that way.

How do you approach the job of publishing?

I don't know if I could articulate that well because I'm still learning. I think of the mag as a schoolroom for myself and my editors. I do appreciate and am interested most of all in the American Scene. We are Americans, you know; I say this without flag-waving. The writers and poets in the new American Scene can teach me more about what it's like to be alive today. The other criterion for accepting a manuscript is one that most any editor would subscribe to: namely, if the writing strikes me as coming out of the man's life and is genuine and articulate, and this artist is telling us some of the truths about the human condition. I prefer the New American lit above the current European work because I want to learn who I am and I want my editors to learn, too, and our readers.

What would you say was the reason for the current renaissance in the American arts—if there is one?

Some of the reason might be psychological in a very profound cultural sense. I'm guessing here—ask me in ten years. We have just fought and suffered through the Second World War, which germinates a terrible kind of nihilism. Since we have no values in this country, as you know, the new American writing is an attempt among the writers to find again: Who am I? It's a very powerful literature that's being written right now.

What do you think the effect of this will be?

Nothing but good. There are no answers among these writers, at least as far as I am able to discern: no cultural statements like in the 30's or even the 20's when you get a great poet like Eliot chanting the doom of the West. In the 30's you get hard-bitten, social, proletariat, political facts kind of literature. None of that exists in the 50's or in the early 60's. Instead, there is a terrible search and an attempt at almost brute honesty, the artist confronting himself, asking: Who am I? Out of these personal statements I think something very positive can come. These are men establishing themselves as being alive. There's nothing very grandiose or religious, even, in their work. It's something very concrete, very American.

What do you think the range of this new poetry is?

All the way from a very domestic, close-to-the-bone poetry (like Robert Creeley, John Logan, W. D. Snodgrass) to a social poetry (like some of Ginsberg's best or Corso or Ferlinghetti). It ranges all the way from a very personal document to an attempt at a commentary on the American cultural and political scene.

What about the audience?

They're fairly young, primarily University-educated, out in the professions in one way or another, without any value, looking for some, searching for their own lives: I think they learn from these writers who talk very directly and very powerfully to them.

What is your poetic aesthetic?

I don't know any more. I was born and raised a Roman Catholic and it gets into your imagination. I used to think that poems were kind of telegrams from angels—like from another world. I really felt that very deeply. Now I don't believe that. My own poems are attempts, the only way I have, to make sense out of my own existence and the world around me and to understand who I am and what my friends are involved in.

Poetry is a way of knowing, really; the only way accessible to me. It is an articulation of what I think is basically chaos: a cat goes by, a dog dies, a woman screams, there's an airplane overhead—that's life and to me it's chaos. I think of a poem as chaos being made concrete, for a moment, in time. Poems are signposts for poets and I hope for other people, too. If the poet speaks the truth of what he is and what his experience has been—good, bad or indifferent—I think his poem will have meaning for other people. A poem is a tongue for the mute hearts of people.

Paul Blackburn

Blackburn has published only three slim books of poetry, (the latest is *The Nets,* issued by Trobar Press), and one of translation, which does not do justice to his large output in both these categories. Fortunately, however, he is widely published in the little magazines and his poems and translations have been frequently anthologized. He has recently been the poetry Editor of *The Nation.*

Part of your academic background can be seen in Proensa *and in your other translations from various languages, especially Provençal. What was the appeal of this period for you?*

What got me started on Provençal was reading squibs of it in the *Cantos* and not being able to understand it, which annoyed me. It hadn't been taught at Wisconsin since the 30's, so I found Professor Bottke, the medievalist out there, who offered to tutor me in it. I needed the course for credit, and to give credit he needed five students. I got him eight and we had a very good course.

Is this why you went to Spain and France later?

That started me. I'd been studying mostly English literature, with French as a minor, along with Greek and Latin and Anglo-Saxon—all that jazz. When the Provençal sort of arrived with me, I followed through and got a Fulbright—after three tries—and there I was.

Paul Carroll has told how he visited you and how you took

his poems apart line by line, "showing how the line breaks according to its own breath, and how a stanza should be built only out of its own unique life." He said, "Blackburn knows his craft. I don't suppose any poet our age handles a single line, a stanza, a whole poem with his skill and grace." What is the importance of this kind of construction to your work?

I think what Paul meant about the stanza and, I suppose, about the whole poem, is that one of the most important things about a poem is that it is basically a *musical* structure and, of course, like any piece of music, it needs resolution. It depends on how you're going at the particular poem—one doesn't always write in the same style, certainly. But to make it work for itself, not only in terms of whatever materials and whatever is trying to be said, it must tie together as a musical unit—however irregular it looks on the page, and even if it sounds almost free-form.

Kerouac, for instance, borrows jazz forms a good bit, and with a fair amount of success in terms of that kind of music, I think. In *Mexico City Blues,* when he reads three or four choruses together, they work in terms of a poem, and will balance out. Some carry material over and some don't. I think it's an interesting concept. It's not the easiest—but Kerouac works the form very well. I don't know anyone, aside from Roi Jones, who even touches on that kind of thing at all.

In what musical terms do you see your poetry?

Mine is probably closer to modern music or, partly, even in the concept of modern jazz. A lot of pieces feel like several instruments or voices—they should, anyway. The point is that a poem has to be resolved musically as well as in terms of its content. Very few people have very consistently good ears. Some of them have ears for small pieces, some for large, some can work in between the two. For instance, Bob Creeley writes mostly small poems—on the whole, fairly short—although recently they've been getting a good bit longer, and I'm glad to see that he's able to sustain his music for a longer period of time. I've always felt that he "got done" too fast. Then, on the opposite extreme, there's Ginsberg. I walked in one day—down there on Second Street—and asked him how things were going. He said, "I started writing a poem to my mother yesterday; it's fifty pages long already. What am I going to do?" That's quite the opposite extreme, where his drive apparently makes not only for a very long line, but often for a very long poem. Olson seems to work between the two things—small structures inside, but longer overall structures. Everyone works differently, and everyone works according to where he is at the moment too, I suppose.

Do you feel that reading your poems aloud as you write or revise them helps this musical element?

Yes, it's good. What goes into the poem, especially in the last ten years, is very much a matter of speech rhythms and of natural, rather than forced rhythms. That is why a poem will very often seem to have no obvious structure whatsoever—in terms of what is conventionally thought of as form. It just doesn't work out that simply, because the rhythms that you start with and that you have to resolve are very often irregular in themselves, or are more highly charged, simply because they are the way we speak. The thing is to speak carefully.

It started ten years ago with Olson, Creeley, Corman, myself and then the people at Black Mountain picked it up, and apparently the movement came to some sort of explosion with the San Francisco Renaissance. An awful lot of people who came out of that—the so-called Beat poets—are writing very much with speech rhythms; but tremendously long lines and tremendously powerful lines in terms of the build-up of the emotion of the poem. I don't see that there's anyone with this kind of emotional power, one might say even a kind of almost hysterical drive, until you go back to Hart Crane or even to Shelley. But of course, they were working in much more controlled forms.

Is the use of "common speech" the most common link between the new poets?

Yes, I think that's probably, in one degree or another, what anyone who is doing anything at all is doing—actually using the language that we use everyday to make their poems with. I think that is one reason why readings in coffeeshops and bars and to friends have become so much more common in the last five years. Poetry is less removed from its audience, if you like.

We had some difficulty finding poems to read for radio broadcast because many of yours contain the words that used to be called "unprintable." Can you explain your extensive usage of such words?

Well, if you want to start from the point of view that speech, and that common speech even, is a very fair and valid medium for poetry, you're going to find some people whose common speech is commoner than most. That would include a lot of the male members—ladies usually watch their language fairly carefully, and that's only right, too.

Certain words will carry the emotion and drive it home more strongly if used well in their context, so to speak. Many of the emotions in poetry are very violent ones. If one is writing a violent poem, one uses violent words. To make the point Lawrence did in the introduction to *Lady Chatterly's Lover*, these words are honest words and they don't really shock you. They shock only if you are willing to be shocked. The words and the parts and functions exist, and if they are out there in the text they are much cleaner and more open, with no suppression and no veiling. The hiding of it, and the skirting of it, can be more suggestive than the outright statement.

Is there one thing more than any other that moves you to write a poem?

No—not one thing. I suppose that one has certain ideas about the world one lives in and the kind of life one leads (or is forced to lead, or would like to lead). Very different things can strike one in terms of a poem. Put a person in varied landscapes or cityscapes and he is surrounded by life —you find out a lot about the quality of the city or the country and the quality of the person. This is very valid material for poetry. What else is there? The man in what surrounds him. That he loves or hates, or just hears and sees.

Jerome Rothenberg

Jerry Rothenberg was caught for an interview before he had thoroughly formulated his conviction in the "deep image." As a result, he has provided comments on his early statements between brackets in the text. His books are *White Sun Black Sun*, (Hawk's Well) and *Seven Hells of the Jigoku Zoshi*, (Trobar). His magazine-anthology *Poems From the Floating World* continues publication.

How did you happen to start the Hawk's Well Press?

Partly it was accidental. With some other poets, I heard that printing could be done very cheaply in Spain, Gibralter and other European countries. The prices were very good compared to what it would cost to print books over here, and we felt like taking advantage of it. Then, gradually, certain ideas grew for us and we formulated a particular direction for the press—the press' character grew out of what concerned us in our writings. We began looking for new poetry that would link up with a meaningful modern tradition, as we understood it. The poets involved as publishers were myself, David Antin and Seymour Faust; later, myself and Armand Schwerner.

What about the anthology, Poems from the Floating World?

I try in that publication to show the inter-relation between poetry written by some young poets in America today and some of the major aspects of European poetry—that poetry, in some sense, is transnational and transtemporal; that certain ways of poetic "seeing"—for example, what I've been calling "deep image"—are keys to the poetry of other times and places, as well as source of power in our own.

We try to have everything as readable as possible, to show that modern European poetry and the archaic and/or primitive poetry to which it's spiritually linked can, for all its difference, be translated into American terms. I feel that, through this translation, we can indicate that the *general* path which American poetry has been taking is not the only path for poetry written in the English, or American, language. But also that "deep image" poetry, to call it that again, has been and continues to be written in America; but that should be obvious or one wouldn't bother.

What do you think the relationship between these European and Latin American poets and the younger American poets is?

The assumption behind this answer is that American poetry has been characterized by structural avant-gardism, and "European" by imagistic (though not in Ezra Pound's sense of image) avant-gardism. This is a general thing and discounts apparent crossovers, and so on.

I think their work has a relationship to that of some of the young American poets writing today, at least to some work by any single poet. I don't think that a full-fledged "movement" representing their kind of poetry exists today in this country, though I have a feeling something is being born today (or re-born) which links up with the major post-Surreal poetry in Europe. [Post-Surreal's a sloppy word, but let it go; a long explanation would be silly. The thing I felt "being born" was an American poetry of the "deep image," explorations of an area hardly touched here and now sighted in our own terms. I still feel it "being born."]

Why do you translate?

First, there's the same pleasure that one gets out of writing poetry in general. But it's a somewhat different process. You have a poem in another language, which takes the place of an immediate inspiration out of a life experience. In a way, I do look at it as being the same kind of life experience, as I would say too that all poets "translate" things and experiences into words, to apprehend them in a sense no longer foreign but accessible as something of one's own.

Also, I began to translate from some sense of dissatisfaction with the kind of poetry that was being written in this country several years ago and, I suppose, even today. I was trying to see what certain poems would read like in my own language. I wanted to have them in front of me. I wanted to see how they worked, how the "other" sensibility worked in English. I think it works out well, and if it does, this again indicates to me that it's possible to have in this country a poetry of fullness and a poetry of deep imagination. I think there are many good poets who use a method of "stripping away" in writing. A poet like Robert Creeley, for example, who speaks about the necessity he feels, as a New Englander, to "travel light" in writing his poetry. But I think the other thing is possible. I think it's been underplayed, and that the position of the "strippers" has tended to hide the real possibilities of this other kind of poetry in English.

[At the time, I was in a long correspondence with Creeley and the point seemed more clearcut than it does now. Part of any good poet's meaning is to be found in what he discards, what he can't use because it isn't "real" for him. Maybe it's a question of degree, how much you're finally able to make real, not just include but make real: but poetry without any subtraction would seem to me now to be powerless to discover or create the "real."]

There seem to be more and more poets who find translation not an academic labor, but a very important part of their craft. Do you agree?

I think we're entering into a major period of translation, as long as it's the poet who does the translation, and as long as the effort with living poetry is to re-create poems in one's own language. There is a value in the literal translation, but I think the primary concern has to be, as with one's own work, the creation of poems—not a slavishness to the cultural boundaries of another person's language. There are things which simply won't stand up when presented literally, without re-creation, because we think differently, because we have a different world about us. Part of this difference has to come through in the translations. It's not just a substitute. Frost spoke of poetry being what gets lost in translation, which is parly true, but I don't believe he ever did translation himself. Sometimes poetry gets found in translation. Goethe, I believe, said the opposite, that the poetry was what came across in translation. It's possible, isn't it, that they were both wrong.

What is your poetic aesthetic?

I think that what I'm looking for is a kind of poetry that will probe deep, in terms of statement and through images, without being untransmittable. I always want to be direct in speaking, although I realize that I'm not dealing with material that, on the face of it, seems to be direct. I don't think that in learning from movements like Surrealism, (to name one that everybody knows; I'm, God knows, not a Surrealist), one has to get into a kind of dense murky poetry which doesn't communicate itself.* I think that somehow, miraculously, what the Surrealists and the post-Surrealists, (but more precisely, those who began to explore a kind of "deep image" from, say, Rimbaud or Whitman on), hit on was not a poetry which obscures communication, but a poetry of the most direct communication possible. That is, an exploration of the unconscious region of the mind in such a way that

* Editor's Note: For other views on Surrealism *vs.* the Image, see the next two conversations. Rothenberg, Kelly and Bly are generally considered, personally and by way of their magazines, the leading agitators for a poetry based on "Image." Robert Creeley also comments on "deep image" in his conversation, recorded about a year after this one.

the unconscious is speaking to the unconscious. If the reader just gives this a chance, the poetry will communicate itself in the most direct terms imaginable. I'm convinced of this in reading other poets and in seeing the effect of poems that I've written on others who come to them almost cold. The communication is possible and it's quite important.

What do you write about?

The effort is to draw things from myself, to draw from things that I've experienced, including the images in my mind and the words I speak, to draw from objects that have a real meaning for me at the deepest level I can reach. Not simply facts, but *real* meanings, assigned values, states of being to be re-experienced or created in the poem. To dredge this up, and in dredging it up, actually to create the poem rather than only to create an artifact. The artifact comes second, and the poem, in a sense, is the material of the Self, material of which the Self has taken possession, which one dredges up to begin with. Sometimes, in writing a poem, you may return to dredge things up again. This isn't like "automatic" writing, which too often just hits the surface of things. I don't feel the first thing one comes to is necessarily the last word, though I do feel that the good poem probably has always come very quickly in its essential form, and that the rest has been the building of an artifact out of it.

[I suppose that here I was reacting to the simple equation of poem with artifact. In working with early or archaic poetry, one is clearly aware that the poet is, to begin with, one with the priest and the shaman, not only "making" but "seeing." Making, in the purely craft sense, seems a later idea, in societies where the poet's experience has become separated from the total experience of the community. "Creator" seems a better translation for poet than "maker," because it implies the greater possibilities that have been present from the beginning. As for the distinction between artifact and poem, let's better say that when they happen, they happen best together, when what we "make" is also what we "see."]

One of the central images in your work seems to be the duality of things. Is this an important concept?

I think that there's a question of bringing things together. One is juxtaposing images, which is to say, juxtaposing objects as the mind apprehends them. One brings together things out of different realms. This is part of the act of creation (when one is left free to create). Yes, I think that something resembling duality would enter there. I hesitate to speak of duality as something accepted or denied; the poem seems to do both. It's a yoking together of things that, to the conscious mind perhaps, never should have been yoked together. Part of the meaning comes through that.

Robert Kelly

Kelly is the co-editor of *Trobar* and Trobar Books and the author of *Armed Descent*, published by Hawk's Well Press in 1961. Since then, his poetry has found print in many magazines, including *Origin*, which devoted most of its fifth issue to "The Exchanges" and other poems. He is presently a literature instructor at Bard College, up the Hudson from his Brooklyn birthplace.

First of all, what is the relationship of the "Image" to Trobar?

With our first issue, we wanted poetry that qualified by being alive in one sense or another. We, in our own work and in our critical attention, grew more and more involved with the poetry of images.

Let me say this about the Image; if you want to divide all the ways of going into the poem, all the quanta and quotients of poetry, I think the division of powers that Ezra Pound made long ago, into three, is the best. His division was: *logos*, or word—word-magic, word-development, the development of meaning; *melos*, the musical gist, the musical development—singing, really—sound; and third, *phanos*, literally, "brightness," phanopeia equalling, for Pound, "throwing the image onto the mind." This is the intellectual and emotional tone of the poem.

Now, if poetry deals with word, word is its ground—you might call word the mystical hypostasis of all poetry, of all literary art. At the same time, music (*melos*) is the space-time of poetry—its line, extent, duration. These two approaches to poetry, or these two behaviors of poetry, have been well analyzed and well discussed for a number of years—I should say about 2500 years at least. The third, *phanos*, the image, has gotten rather slighting attention. In the 30's and 40's we heard a lot about "metaphor," largely, I suppose because Pound was talking about metaphor in the 10's and 20's; but we've also heard a little about image.

The image poetry that I'm talking about is not what Pound nowadays means when he speaks of the poetry *des Amy-gistes*. When I speak of Image Poetry, I'm speaking both of a way of looking at all poetry, and also, in our own time, of a particular stance of the poet as regards his material; that stand generates a kind of poetry not necessarily dominated by the images, but in which it is the rhythm of images which form the dominant movement of the poem. I'm not trying to say that all great poetry is essentially Image Poetry. I will say that all great poetry generates its images, both the Final Emergent Image of the work of art (Pound calls the *Commedia* a single image), and more so, the image as prime generated material of the poem—the primal image—which can be expressed as it normally is—in the word—but can also be expressed, can cohere in, sound.

Now this all seems rather remote from *Trobar,* but what I've been saying records part of the sharpening process that went on in my mind and in the minds of my friends and associates. This sharpening of focus led us to try to make *Trobar* a vehicle for Image Poetry. I certainly don't say that that's the only place it can be found, or the only place it will be found, because the poetry of image is coming more and more to life in America. For confirmation, don't look to any tendentious little magazine whatever, but to the work itself or more and more poets. I think the revival of interest in poets like Lorca and Neruda—they're becoming almost "standard" poets now—is based very largely on the enormous dark sentiment of Lorca, that darkness that "surrounds" us in *things,* and on Neruda's celebrations and love of the things of the earth. In their work, image becomes the motive force of the poem: their voice is in the images, as much as in the music.

If they play, they play on some ground. Really, this revival had to come, this awakening to the fulness of poetry, after the dry wit and tricks of words that marred so much of the poetry of the 50's. This is a partisan statement, but the worst thing you can say about a poem, any poem, is that it's dull.

Do you think that a poetry concerned with the Image is likely to be a surrealist kind of poetry?

I think probably the first stage an individual poet would go through in trying to let image emerge in his work would be a surrealist one. I really don't believe that surrealism and the Poetry of Image necessarily constitute more than a companionate marriage. Surrealism has its own technique at the heart—I think it is a technique—and I feel, rightly or wrongly, that the Poetry of Images (stress on Poetry: it's not a technique) is essentially a mode of Vision. Vision is something of enormous importance in talking about poetry—we very rarely talk about it, perhaps because it's so indefinable. (Pound, for instance, leaves it out altogether in the *ABC of Reading*: that book is so good because it keeps to the discrete: you can't teach the other.) The use of images constitutes a part of the poet's Vision. It has nothing to do with technique. You can simulate a surrealist poem but you cannot simulate, in a true sense, an Image Poem. This is no real criticism of surrealism—it has its own concerns. But if it can be extrapolated and a technique formed on the basis of it, it's not what we're talking about. Image is a vehicle for Vision. Vision discovers. What some consider Blake's fancies are explorations of the real world, discoveries through perception. Remember what Stevens said: Surrealism invents, it cannot discover.

In your recent issue, you publish poems by Creeley, Duncan and Snyder. How does their work in Trobar *differ from their work to be found in other magazines featuring them and the "New American Poetry?"*

I don't believe it differs at all. I want to bring up again

that I don't think that Image Poetry is the only kind of poetry. The poetry we publish, God knows, the poetry we write, is new and it is American; the important thing is that it gets written, that it stands.

I think Duncan is one of the greatest poets writing today in English. I think, as various people, notably Creeley, have said of him, that his work is enormously rich in technical solutions as well as in movement and meaning. I would think very little of a magazine that isolated itself from a poet such as Duncan merely because Duncan operates on all levels of poetic meaning. His *Venice* poem, his greatest work I've encountered, is very strongly built on the flow of Image, as well as upon space and measure.

With Creeley, there's a different consideration. Creeley, too, is an exceedingly fine poet I think, if I can say so without anything at all except humble admiration of the man and his work—a man who's writing poetry of a beauty that I thought, a few years ago, impossible in this day and age—of an excellence I still think incredible. Again, for the magazine, similar reasons apply. Snyder is most relevant as far as the Poetry of Images is concerned. This most recent book of Snyder's, *Myths and Texts*, is in my mind one of the strongest books published by an American since the *Pisan Cantos*, let's say. And it is, by my definition, Image Poetry. That's a tremendously important book, not just as an accomplishment and a measure, but as a direction.

The origin of a paper you have written, called Notes on the Poetry of Images,* *was in seeing Eisenstein films and relating*

---

* The paper referred to was privately circulated. A later version was published as *Notes on the Poetry of Deep Image* in *Trobar* 2, 1961. Before the printed version came out, the author benefitted from a number of comments and criticisms generously and relevantly supplied by many people, especially Robert Duncan, Robert Creeley, Gary Snyder, Denise Levertov (whose critique was published in *The Floating Bear* No. 11) and Charles Olson, whose brief comment: "not imageS but IMAGE," was fundamental. Most of these comments took exception to the terms of the paper or their development: the names given above

the Image in poetry to filmic montage. Do you still see Image Poetry in these terms?

Since then I've thought about something that might be a difference, might not be a difference. The film starts out with a *known* reality: the reality the camera faces—and when you're building up film montage with the sequences and the strips and the cuts and finally the frame itself, I think that you are in a different position altogether from the poet employing images. Different only because, while you don't know what the outcome is going to be, you at least know what you have to start out with. The poet doesn't. There is a Mystery in poetry, and I really mean this with a capital M, a darkness, an atmosphere in which the author composes the Images before he really knows what those Images amount to. Now, if you take one of the famous Eisenstein frames—a long line of troops seen far in the distance across a snowy field—whatever this Image may amount to in later development, it is something in itself. It is white and black and grey and the very thin line of soldiers and the whole horizontal motion—and the motion in depth. You can take it out and print it in a book, look at it and know what you're seeing. It is a thing. The poetic Image is not a thing. It is process and a discovered identity. It discovers its being in its function.

I think there's that difference, and this is really why I bring in the question of rhythm. Image is the rhythm of poetry. I've said this over and over again in my paper, and I must say now, and give full credit, that this is a formulation that is not originally mine, though I've made use of it fully. Nicolas Calas, the Surrealist writer and art critic, offers as a dictum (I really don't know in what context, since I've seen it only quoted) just this statement: "The combination of images

---

are in no way responsible for the printed version, which, it should be noted, paid much less attention to the film. (R. K., 1962)

Editor's Note: My own comments on Kelly's paper, which do pay considerable attention to the film, were also published in *The Floating Bear,* No. 13.

constitutes the rhythm of the poem." Rather than talk of laws of combinations, I just want to say that the Image itself, in its development, constitutes the fundamental, basic rhythm of the poem, which all other rhythms—sound rhythms, stress rhythms and so forth—must subserve.

Now here again I think you come back to the film, with its interspersal of one shot with another and (I don't know what Eisenstein calls it) the visual similarity, if not identity, of two successive images of different subjects—their formal, structural nature being the same. The intertranslatability of all things is fundamental to all poetry: it is perhaps more obvious in Image Poetry, and perhaps there there's a tie-in with the film. If it does tie up with film montage, it does so not so much from the point of view of the individual frame, as from the rhythmic point of view of what is done with the frame. The processes may be analogous; the modular units are different.

Is there any one experience, more than another, that prompts you to write a poem?

It's something that I do. I don't know how to stop writing them. I don't know what the impetus is—or, I guess, we can all say in one theoretical way or another what the impetus is and we all know in one real way or another what the impetus is, but can we verbalize them? Have any people succeeded in verbalizing that impetus? The conformation of necessities in the unconscious, the conformation of shapes and structures that demand expression—I think it is that, or sometimes the song—the sound of music of some kind.

Robert Bly

Bly talked with me in the spring of 1960, just after the magazine which he edits with William Duffy had changed its name from *The Fifties* to *The Sixties*. His first book of poetry is *Silence in the Snowy Fields* (Wesleyan) and he has translated *The Story of Gosta Berling* (New American Library). Translations of Trakl and Vallejo have been published by The Sixties Press.

You have said that "most of the poetry published in America today is too old-fashioned." Why do you think this?

Well, I think that for about 20 or 25 years, American poetry has been out of touch with the current poetry being done in Europe. A certain kind of poetry has grown up there which is able to handle the experiences of modern life, including war and advertising and so on, better than any American poets have been able to do. This is not from a lack of experience, so it must be from a lack of a way to *approach* this experience. My conviction is that poetry in the English and American languages has been tied down too much to the kind of poetry coming from Eliot and John Donne and others—poetry which loses itself in forms and which is too conscious of the English tradition.

What do you feel has been the effect of the so-called Beat poets, or the "New American Poets?"

I think they have done a good deal to break the stronghold of Academic poetry. I think, however, that this poetry itself is old-fashioned. The way they put together a poem is basically the way a poem was put together in the nineteenth century: making very direct statements and talking directly and specifically about the subject matter.

The kind of poetry that has been developed in Europe and South America is a poetry in which the image comes forward and much more is said by suggestion. The subconscious and the unconscious are brought forward in the poetry, and the poem doesn't hang so much on observed fact and thing as the poetry of the Beats does.

You have also said that "we have had no bold new poetry" since about 1922. Why do you think poetry in America has been "dry?"

English and American poetry has not had a period of surrealism. The English poets, if this is mentioned, will usually say: "Well, that's because we're really so much superior to the French. The French are very rational people and therefore they need surrealism." The English are morons. My opinion is that the reason French poetry and Spanish poetry has continued to be fresh and strong in language during the past thirty years is precisely because those languages did go through a period of surrealism—a period of heavy use of imagery from the unconscious, beginning with Baudelaire. This has given their poetry great flexibility and richness and depth. Our poetry, because of its clinging to things and to the surface of life, has tended to become too barren. The language has begun to dry up. Unless English and American poetry can enter, really, an inward depth, through a kind of surrealism, it will continue to become dryer and dryer.

Are there any poets now working in this direction?

I see a few. I personally don't think that a writer like Henry Treece, who is discussed as an English surrealist, really is one. There are several kinds of surrealism. In one sort, you break the structure of the conscious mind, so that the conscious mind is not able to understand the poem. Sometimes in the poetry of Frank O'Hara, John Ashberry and Lamantia, you will find this kind of surrealism—in which the conscious mind is unable to understand what is being said. But, in a sense, this is a negative surrealism, a false surrealism. There is another kind which simply disregards the conscious and the intellectual structure of the mind entirely and, by the use of images, tries to bring forward another reality from *inward* experience. I see a few young writers using this: James Wright has broken abruptly, and is writing a kind of poetry which resembles that of Cesar Vallejo and Pablo Neruda. Other young poets—I think Jerome Rothenberg has written three or four poems which involve a true surrealism.

Has this any relation to "automatic" writing?

No. None at all. I think the major misunderstanding in America has been the association of surrealism completely with French surrealism. It's interesting that Garcia Lorca, who wrote a great deal of surrealist poetry, had the feeling that French surrealism was not true surrealism. He felt that their investigation of automatic writing was merely a rational thing, and that in most cases, French poetry was not able to break through rationality. He felt that French poetry, after the period of Rimbaud, had begun to die, and that the true surrealism of his time was appearing in the Spanish language. I still think this is true. We have a warped view of surrealism because of our exclusive concentration on the French language. Their surrealism was a surrealism, but a fairly narrow channel of that surrealism.

You translate a great deal. Why do you feel that translation is so important?

This is the real way that poetry in a given language remains fresh—by receiving stimulation and suggestion constantly from other languages. Assuming that my speculation is correct— that American poetry is in a poor state relative to poetries in other languages—one of the reasons certainly is that our translation for the past thirty years has been very weak and very poor. None of the poets that are really well known have spent their lives in translation, whereas the Nobel Prize winner Quasimodo's work is over half translation. The same is true of Pasternak. Americans have felt themselves so powerful and so strong in the world that they really have a kind of superiority complex, even in poetry, toward other nations. We tend not to translate seriously.

John Logan

Logan, a professor at Notre Dame, is the author of two books: *Cycle for Mother Cabrini* (Grove) and *Ghosts of the Heart* (University of Chicago). These two presses should give fair indication of the range of his work. His magazine, *Choice,* continues publication in Chicago.

Having written a good deal of it yourself, how do you feel about religious poetry?

I very much dislike pious, sentimental, sticky poetry of which there is a good deal published in poor magazines, but it seems to me that religious themes need and deserve good, powerful treatment. It happens that my second book had many fewer poems on specifically religious themes in it. I made a statement for that book which I'd like to read:

"A poet is a priest or necromancer of the baroque who dissolves by the incantations of his cadenced human breath the surface of the earth to show under it the covered terror, the warmth, the formal excitement and the gaudy color-burst of the sun. This is not a chemical function. It is a sacramental one, and John Crowe Ransom is right to call poetry 'the secular form of piety.' 'Miraculism everywhere,' he says. So if some people find my subjects less religious now than they used to be, the reason is that I now think poetry itself more religious than I used to do."

By this I mean the sense of the transformation by art of the natural event into something of beauty and of an enduring transcendent quality, which brings to people a kind of secular grace. This seems to me to be very much the function of a poem. I remember Dylan Thomas talking about a poem as a "temporary peace won out of the harsh reality," and this seems to me a kind of religious-like theme. That's why I like Ransom's term "a secular form of piety." So in this sense, it seems to me that every successful poem involves a kind of religious process.

Do you mean a process of belief?

No, I don't mean that so much as one in which elementary materials are transformed, in a higher way, as a result of the impact of art. Henry Miller's statement is very striking in this regard—he said something to the effect that the work of the artist was to take the sour dough of humanity and make this into bread and the bread into wine and the wine into song. And this seems to the point. It's a notion of art quite close to James Joyce's also, I think. Joyce used religious terms like "Epiphany" to describe what he thought was going on in art. An Ephiphany is the showing forth, under a special artistic light, of a human event.

Paul Carroll told me that when he was young he used to think poetry was "telegrams from angels," but now that he's older, he no longer believes that. . . .

The idea of receiving an inspiration—an angel's telegram —is a sort of passive notion. It's a very old one, of course. That sounds like Paul talking—and to say that he no longer does . . .

How do you, as an academician, feel about the current revolt against the "academic" in poetry?

That's like your question about the religious in poetry. It has to be good and it can't be dull. If academic themes in poetry means something pedantic, textbookish, the poem's not going to live.

I don't care how much Chicago is against academic themes or the academic notion in poetry. I'm not against any kind of poetry that is good and I feel a pretty strong sense in some of those people who supposedly are in such revolt that they can't get into the magazines which print such poems. I do agree with Karl Shapiro wholeheartedly when he talks about the notion that poetry has to be taught in its own time. He says that our time is the first in which we've had this idea of poetry. I think that this is quite right. You have a sense sometimes that the academic poet writes the poems in order to have them taught to somebody. This is ridiculous. The sense of the creative in the poem has no such bounds upon it.

But—if getting rid of the academic in poetry means getting rid of literary allusion, for example, then I am, in some of my most recent poems, still quite academic. I don't see why we have to chop off any kind of experience or expression in poetry and say that they can't be used any more. Let's keep anything that's good. Some of my poems are academic in the sense that they use heavy literary allusion, but even when they do, I want there to be present sufficient surface feelings that the poem gets a response from the reader without whole knowledge of the pattern of allusion.

Gilbert Sorrentino

Gil Sorrentino's first book, *The Darkness Surrounds Us,*
was published in 1960 by Jonathan Williams. *Neon,* which
had just ceased publication at the time we had this conversation, has not been revived, but Sorrentino did serve as
guest Editor for *Kulchur* 4. He lives and works in New York
City.

How did you happen to start Neon?

I suppose the way everyone else starts a little magazine, or
most of the people I'm aware of. It usually comes about
through purely selfish motives. I don't mean that pejoratively
—by selfish I mean that one thinks he knows people who are
doing writing of value, and these people are not being published as often as they should be published, or they're not
being published at all. So the first issue of a little magazine
is usually devoted to those people that the editor knows and
believes in.

Did the magazine catch on, sell, become successful?

Neon was never successful. It had its audience of roughly
two hundred people, and that's about all I wanted, actually.
I have maybe a personal feeling about a magazine, not shared
by everyone who edits or publishes, which is: the people that
I want to see the magazine, I know *will* see the magazine.
Things are that tight.

It comes to the point that a man can come from San Francisco or Chicago or Denver or any of a number of cities and

towns in the United States, to New York, and within a week a writer will know just about every other writer in New York City. It's that tight. You know that he has seen your publication somehow. If he hasn't bought it, someone has loaned it to him. There's a very loose rapport among poets today and nobody is very much impressed by the fact that somebody else is a poet. One is impressed by the work shown. At any rate, that's my particular attitude toward things. Most of the people I know are poets—it just happens to be hopelessly true. But I suppose that eventually happens—you live in a hermetic society. The fact that they're poets doesn't fill me with awe; I'm filled with awe over their work, if it's good. And there are a lot of very good poets working today.

It's really a beautifully amazing thing that a little magazine which can look so hopelessly inadequate can reach so many people who care. By "care," I speak really of a writers' audience in this situation, which is what just about every writer has today. It's sad to say in one way, and in another way I think it's good. An audience *per se* has ceased to exist for the American writer. The once fairly well-to-do middle class, that took its entertainment by reading something worthwhile, no longer takes its entertainment that way. So you find that your audience usually consists either of other writers, or people who are intensely interested in what is happening in, let's say, the avant-garde world of letters; it's been like that, I'd say, since just before the First World War. The little magazine is literally the *little* magazine in every way.

So then, Neon *failed for financial reasons?*

That's one of the reasons. The point being that the money I would lay out to publish the magazine I never got back in return. I couldn't hope to even break even. That's why I felt that I had to let it go as a regular publication.

In the Donald Allen anthology, you are included in the "unaffiliated" section. With whom do you think you are affiliated?

I think Don was doing what is certainly the fine thing to do with that particular breakdown or delineation of the poets in the book. His idea was that you have to make people understand that the new poets are not a bunch of illiterate, barbaric, slightly criminal types.

I'm certainly not a member of the Black Mountain group, mainly because I never went to Black Mountain College. I'm not a member of the Beat group, mainly because I'm not "beat." Besides, I don't really believe the "Beat Movement" is any longer a movement—most of the Beat poets have been assimilated into the general tenor of what is going on today. My own writing, I suppose you would say, if you wanted to say it was close to something, is certainly close to the Black Mountain group. My major influence has been Robert Creeley's work. He was definitely a member of that group and is, if it still exists. He is the man who more or less showed me what to do.

I had come out of Pound, and then certainly Williams; but Williams leads to something in his own poems which comes directly out of his mind—that is, his poems take the shape of his mind. Naturally, each poet's mind is different, and my mind is not so closely attuned to Williams that I could completely use his work as an influence. I read *The Whip* in 1957 or so—a small, selected group of poems from Creeley's earlier books—and *The Whip* had me jumping up and down. It gave me what I would consider a direction.

What would you consider that direction to be?

It was a matter, I suppose you could say, of the "oblique" in poetry. Coming into a subject at an angle instead of approaching it directly. Instead of seizing on those things which are salient in a subject, one comes in at an angle and reveals things in a subject which are usually not revealed with the direct approach. It's something that was probably brought to its peak of perfection in a different language when Mallarmé was writing his poems.

Now, when I say "oblique," I don't mean "oblique" in the quality of the language—Creeley's language is razor-sharp. There's no doubt what Creeley is ever saying. It's the combination of words which makes the poem which I call oblique. In other words, it's the direction-force of the poem *into* a subject. Creeley's attack on the subject is from an angle. He reveals the subject from his own particular way of looking at it, and that is what is so unique about his work; that is why he is to me certainly one of the three or four most important poets working today, (and the youngest of the three or four that I think of).

The attack of, let's say, Ginsberg is just—I won't say just, I don't mean that in a corny sort of contemptuous way at all —it's merely that Ginsberg feels that he must reveal the subject in every facet. "I saw the best minds of my generation destroyed by madness, starving hysterical naked"—there is no room for doubt there; you know exactly what Ginsberg says.

And he says it over and over again, so that very often you lose the specific impacts of the poem . . .

It's what I like to call the "spray technique." It's not a technique at all—I just like to think of it that way in my mind. It's an approach to a subject in which one fires at the subject with, as it were, buckshot. Some of the pellets must hit the subject. The pellets which don't hit the subject? Well, that's just unfortunate. Of course the pellets, being the words, stay on the page and tend to dull or muddy what is being spoken of. Whereas Creeley hits the subject in the center, he fires one bullet—his misses are the poems that don't make it. But you know when they don't make it, or eventually you will find out what is the better Creeley, et cetera.

Speaking of the great influential poets of our time, Olson is certainly Creeley's mentor, I would say. Everyone else in the world today who cares for poems has learned from Olson. Olson is our Ezra Pound, if you want to be very corny about it. He is the oldest of the group, and he is the one man in the group who has written a long poem which makes it—*The Maximus Poems*—a beautiful book in which, on every level, mastery is shown.

What moves you to write a poem?

An idea. A feeling.

An intellectual thing, rather than an object in the visual world?

You can't say it's one thing or the other. It's the way perhaps every poet writes a poem. One sees something or becomes aware of something, and something occurs in the brain in which you see the possibilities for a poem. A poem becomes possible, dealing with that particular thing, and then all that remains to do is write it. In other words, the feeling or the thought that has come out of the particular feeling that has come into you, has to find its shape. This shape is the poem. You don't take what you feel or what you've thought about what you've felt and try to gild that with words. What you do is try to put that thing *into* words. The words are the shape of the feeling; a poem is itself—it doesn't deal with anything, it's not about anything. It *is* something.

What intellectual controls govern your work?

Once I decide to write the poem, then everything that I know about the technique of writing a poem—the tools that I can use—comes into play. That's why, of course, each poet is different, because each poet uses his tools in a different way. A man who knows nothing of the technique of writing poems can have, let's say, the essentials of genius in him, but he won't be able to write a decent poem (unless some kind of miracle occurs) *unless* he knows his trade. It would be as if a man had a beautiful sculpture in his mind—without knowing how to sculpt, he would make a botch of the piece of material he was sculpting. I have seen paintings in my own mind, but I can't paint a line. I don't know how to paint. All I know about painting is that you put the paint down and something occurs. But I don't know how to handle the paint. It's the same with a man handling his words. You've got to know your trade, you've got to go to school, you've got to go to your betters.

I think it must begin with being a painter or a poet. You can't help the drive. From there you go on to the learning and the influences . . .

Of course. You don't just consciously say, "Today I'm going to write a poem." It's just that you can't help writing the poem. You must write the poem whether it come out bad or good. It's something that bothers you until it's written out of you. Nine out of every ten poems I write I just chuck— dump them out.

Do you rework your poems a great deal? It has seemed to me that Ginsberg represents a certain lack of the editorial "blue-pencil" sense . . .

That could be. Allen has always annoyed me because, of all that group of so-called Beat poets, his is an outstanding intelligence, and it constantly annoys me that he allows himself to be used. Certainly not used by other poets, but by the people who have always hated poetry—the vested interests, the commercialists, the buyers and sellers. Ginsberg can talk for an hour about how he loathes *Life, Time, Fortune,* money, banking, and *Life* and *Time* will spread-eagle him on the wall with his own words. His words don't have the power to destroy *Life* and *Time.* That's why he gets so much space in them and one of the reasons he is so used by them. He's not an enemy of *Life* and *Time*—he *is* an enemy in his own heart, as every poet must be—but they're not afraid of him and they make the fool of him.

It's very peculiar. It's a reversion to Romanticism. It's the Romantic scream against the watered-down principles of

Locke, which controlled the 19th century. As the Romantics screamed against Locke, they made Locke righter. The more they said "Down With Locke," in so many different ways: "I fall upon the thorns of life, I bleed," et cetera, the more they continually made Locke seem right. Locke was wrong. But they didn't prove it so. He said, or he was taken to have said, when his philosophy was watered down a hundred years later, as philosophies always are for the people, "Poetry is junk—evanescent, something to curl up with on a winter's evening. It has nothing to do with life." The old cry of the businessman. So the Romantics said, "That's right, Locke, you bet it is." And they just kept screaming about the wild blue yonder. It wasn't until the 19th century Frenchmen that poetry once again became what it is—something having to do directly with life, something that can be used to control your life, something that can be used to make your life a better thing. They got back to the concrete, they got back to the world that Locke accused them of rejecting.

Don't you think many of the contemporary poets are Romantics themselves?

Sure. All the Beats are Romantics. Every single Beat alive is a Romantic. They're Romantics in the worse sense—they're ego-mad, they think that whatever they say about themselves other people will be interested in. It's not true. No one is interested in the "I" of the poem, unless that "I" is projected through a mask. Yeats has taught us that. These people haven't gone to school—that's their great trouble. Except for Allen and that's what bugs me about Allen, because he knows this and rejects it in his own work.

The Romantics failed art. They failed art a hundred years ago. Pound, Williams, Wyndham Lewis, T. S. Eliot, Ford Madox Ford, Joyce, spent their lives destroying a decayed structure. Now, sixty years after the groundwork that they laid down, we're erecting another decayed structure on top of it with this neo-Romantic kind of burble.

It's the "I" poem: "I think this and I am that"—without having the objectivity of the e-y-e eye, only the subjectivity of the capital I . . .

Of course. Creeley writes "I" poems, in which he says, "I did this and I did that," but that isn't Creeley speaking—that's Creeley-as-poet speaking. That's Creeley, who might as well say, "*One* did this and *one* did that." It isn't the "I" of Creeley. Creeley doesn't tell you a true-confession story. Creeley uses the "I" as Yeats used the "I"—as a projection from a mask. That's the only way you can sustain the so-called lyric, or, let's say, the lyric in the sense of first person singular. You can't sustain the lyric if you're going to talk *really* about yourself. That's Ginsberg's trouble, that's Corso's trouble, that's Bremser's trouble.

The "I" poem is dangerous only if you forget that you must use the "I" with discretion. In *Projective Verse*, Olson says that we have got to forget that we are men. In other words, he asks why a poet, why any human being, should think that he is more important than other objects in the world. The poet's job is to delineate the objects in the world. The poet's job is not to take that door over there and lay on that door what his idea of that door is. The poet's job is to reveal the door in its essence. Everything has its signature, everything is as important as everything else to the poet—or should be. Once the poet believes that he is more important than the other objects that walk or stand upon the earth, he begins writing "I" poems, which are of interest to no one. It's dangerous to lay this down as a rule though, because there are many poets who have told you about their lives and who've done it with consummate artistry. Villon, certainly. Of course, nobody yet knows who Villon was, or if he was exactly what he said he was, but the point is that all his poems are "I" did this and "I" did that. It's rescued because nowhere does Villon take on the omniscience that one sometimes finds in the poet who constantly says, "I am this and I want to do that." Your eye must be on a level with the other objects that are spoken of in the poem—the "I" cannot be omniscient—that can't happen. If it does, you have a faulty book.

You've got to know your place as a poet in the world—all you are is someone who reveals the essence of things. If you feel that your essence is worth revealing, then that's got to be done with absolute artistry, or its a failure. Even the so-called Beat poets, whose ideas and aesthetics I have no truck with whatsoever, have gradations among them—there are good ones and bad ones. There are people who aren't in the Allen anthology who are good poets and who happen just not to be in the book for one reason or another. They have their own aesthetics and those aesthetics can be traced.

Certainly all of us come right out of Pound. I mean, we're all made possible by Pound. Pound is the master of all of us writing. If it weren't for Pound, we'd be doing something else—we'd probably be writing, but God knows what.

Just what, in your opinion, has been Pound's influence?

Pound, almost singlehandedly, back before the First World War, around 1905, just before his first book came out, freed the language from its artificiality. Essentially, that's what Pound did. The language was draped in the unnecessary, it was ridden with abstract nouns. People were constantly talking, in their poems, about Fate and Death and Life. Pound spoke of things before the eye. He brought things back to the concrete, which the poem has always been, or should be. The poem should deal with the concrete—what one can see, what one can touch, what one can hold. If it doesn't, it usually will fail, because a poet's job is not to talk about the abstract —the poet's job is to talk about the world he lives in. Pound made that possible, along with other men who worked with him. Pound is the major figure, because not only was his aesthetic correct in that sense, but he was the greatest technician of his time. His ear was and is to this very day, absolutely perfect. He has the finest ear of any man writing today. The only poet that I've ever read whose ear approximates Pound's is Shakespeare. I would say that Yeats didn't have the ear of Pound. Mainly those things are what has made Pound our master—that and the fact that his criticism is the only criticism worth reading, almost, outside of Williams and whatever Ford wrote. Certainly, Pound's is the major body of criticism written about the work that was done between, let's say, 1915 and 1940 which is worth reading today, which can teach you almost everything that you should know—if you're a poet.

Robert Creeley

Creeley squeezed in this interview on the Saturday morning in May 1961, that he was to leave New York, having only recently returned to the States from Guatamala. He is now a Visiting Lecturer at the University of New Mexico. Scribners published his *For Love: Poems 1950-60* this spring, collecting work from seven previous books. Creeley, who also is a notable prose writer, is presently working on a novel titled *The Island.*

What was it about the atmosphere at Black Mountain College that so influenced the students?

At the time I was there, the College was in very straitened circumstances and had a great deal of difficulty in maintaining its operation, so that I think everyone present felt a curiously useful desperation. It finally proved the end of the College, of course, but I think we all felt a seriousness and an openness of form and intention that was extremely useful to all concerned. The students, I suppose, had a more difficult time than the faculty, although the faculty seems to have had troubles enough, but we were very much concerned with the problems of experimental education and what could be done now. We wanted a kind of teaching that usually depended upon actually being involved in the materials that were being used. So that, for example, in painting or writing, we had people who were painters or writers, as opposed to those who might be more theoretically involved.

Now how that relates to poetry is a more diffuse question. At first there was the hope to publicize the College, and to make people aware that it was continuing, by publishing a magazine. This was, we thought, the most quick and simple manner of telling people we were still alive.

When did the Black Mountain Review *start, actually?*

1954-55, about. I was still in Mallorca, and had been publishing books under the name of the Divers Press, when Charles Olson, who was my very good friend although curiously I'd never met him, suggested I start a magazine, because we happily had the use of cheap printing and also because, through correspondence, I had access to a good many people who were very active. And too, we had Cid Corman's *Origin* to build on, in a sense. So that was the beginning of the *Black Mountain Review.* Shortly after the first issue I went to teach at Black Mountain, and then I left briefly, and then came back again.

I have a little hesitation about the question of "schools." I was reading recently at Goddard College and met the reaction I thought reasonable, "is Donald Allen's anthology simply another instance of a group which is going to prove another exclusion for younger people now trying to find a means and a way in their own terms of poetry?"

So I almost would like—not to bury Black Mountain, because it probably gave me more coherence than I otherwise would have had, certainly that, but I don't like to feel that it's any exclusion, or any ultimate purpose or form or *via* that's finally been settled upon once and for all. We had exceptional students. I was thinking of Edward Dorn and of Mike Rumaker, specifically those two men, who have consequently proved all that anyone ever hoped of them. There were many others of that kind—all the students had that quality of openness and self-determination.

Both students and teachers at Black Mountain seem to write poetry which differs considerably in style from one to the other . . .

I think what did happen then, and what continues to happen among these people to join us all together, is this: a very conscious concern with the manner of a poem, with the form of a poem, so that we are, in that way, freed from any solution unparticular or *not* particular to ourselves. Olson, I believe, was a decisive influence upon me as a writer, because he taught me how to write. Not how to write poems that he wrote, but how to write poems that I write. This is a very curious and very specific difference.

I think of Paul Blackburn, he was really the first poet I ever knew, and I remember arriving in New York in a pretty hysterical fashion—we were about to take one of those boats —and Paul and I spent two and a half days and nights simply talking about *how do you write a poem?* We'd come, very respectfully, from Pound's influence. Pound, again, is back of all this, as is William Carlos Williams. We all had to find the character of our own intelligence, I suppose it would be, our own minds, the terms of our own living, and we did it by this preoccupation with *how is the poem to be put on the page.* Not "how do we feel generally"—are we good people or bad people—but how shall we actually speak to other people in this medium in a way that's not exclusively personal, but in a way that is our own determination.

Certainly this whole group of poets has a profound concern for form, and Olson has written a good deal on the subject. How do you feel about the "beat" poets, and other, younger, writers who seem less concerned with matters of form?

Let me not try to claim Allen Ginsberg for my side, because he's there anyhow. I think I'm on his side certainly. Now Allen made some comments about Whitman's line in a note on a record of his reading of *Howl and Other Poems.* He is a conscious writer. I mean by that, that he is aware of the technical problems of putting words on a page in a consequent or coherent manner. He specifically seems to be intent on handling this long line that Whitman developed in a manner, again, specific to the content that Allen is involved with.

You see, we're all of us, so to speak, somebody. We all of us have a specific emotional issue or term of contact in our lives, so that, in one sense, when someone says, "There's nothing to say," there's almost an impossible amount of things to say from this basic position. In Allen's terms, he comes, of course, from an environment that gives him the use of a kind of litany or ritualistic, chant-like quality of speaking. He also comes from an urbanism. Allen is specific to a history of the growth of a world, I suppose, so that that's something he's got to say.

Most of the Black Mountain poets have, generally, a short, fragmented line and many cast this into a highly structured phrase. In turning from The Whip *to* The Form of Women, *you developed a more lyrical line. I might add that it's curious that some of your poems, with their wry sense of humor, take on the characteristics of a macabre light verse . . .*

Well that's a New England temper you must remember. When things are really impossible, you start laughing—not weakly, the louder the better. In the earlier poems you mention, the emotional terms are very difficult. The poems come from a context that was difficult to live in, and so I wanted the line to be used to register that kind of problem, or that kind of content. Elsewhere I remember I did say that "Form is never more than an extension of content," and by that I meant that the thing to be said will, in that way, determine how it will be said. So that if you're saying, "Go light the fire," "fire" in that registration will have one kind of emphasis, and if you start screaming, "Fire! Fire!" of course that will have another. In other words, the content of what is semantically involved will very much function in how the statement of it occurs. Now the truncated line, or the short, seemingly broken line I was using in my first poems, comes from the somewhat broken emotions that were involved in them. Now, as I begin to relax, as I not so much grow older, but more settled, more at ease in my world, the line can not so much grow softer, but can become, as you say, more lyrical, less afraid of concluding. And rhyme, of course, is to me a balance not only of sounds, but a balance which implies agreement. That's why, I suppose, I'd stayed away from rhymes in the early poems except for this kind of ironic throwback on what was being said.

You have engaged in a considerable correspondence with other poets on the subject of poetic techniques. Do you think that this "talking through letters" has made you an influence upon many of them?

It's been an influence on me. Pound once said that whenever a group of people begin to communicate with one another, something happens. I've learned tremendously from the correspondence with Paul Blackburn, with Denise Levertov, with Charles Olson with whom I had this contact for five years prior to meeting him. As I've said somewhere, Olson was a practical college of information and stimulus for me. I suppose, equally, I've had some contact or influence with others in that same sense. I believe in handing everything over. If I find anything of use, I try to get it as quickly as possible to whomever I consider might use it. Pass it on. Recently, at a college reading again, a student said to me, and I can understand what was meant, "When you hear something you really want to say, don't you in that sense, not want to say it? Because if you say it, then it's gone and you don't have it anymore." Well, in any of these issues I've lived or believed that by such communication I find a life, and perhaps it will be, in no specious sense, of use to others. So if I've had influence, I hope it's been of that kind. In other words, just now, I'm not as yet clear on what's being done with "deep image." But they need a base for writing, and that seems to be theirs for now. Perhaps they will show more than I intend to recognize at the moment.

What do you understand by "deep image?"

It's the question of symbol. I don't want to say "picture" because that's not accurate. It's what is in the poem as a kind of statement in the sense "a house," "a car," "a field"— the image projected by the statement—as opposed to how the statement is registered. I can't really discuss with any responsibility what they are involved with. They seem to come primarily from the French Symbolists—or specifically I think the Surrealists, the German Expressionist writers of the period just around the First World War—Trakl, Gottfried Benn, and now the present German writers who seem to have reasserted that interest. The Spanish writers such as Lorca, Jimenez and Machado, people of this order whose poems are a fabric of images. There's no other adequate word for it, I'm afraid. Lorca was writing, as I understand it, in a very traditionally settled form—either folk ballads or else other forms more developed in the Spanish tradition—so his issue as he wrote was not to change these forms as say, an American poet might now take on that job in his own tradition, but to learn how to use them to carry a content important to himself and finally and even consequently to others. Lorca's primary quality seems the lucidity in his line and this curiously moving image or images which he can carry in his poems. That is what I believe the "deep imagists" are beginning with. They're going much deeper than that—"deep image" is "deep"—ok.

Everytime I see "1945-1960" on the cover of the Allen anthology, I get a slightly apocolyptic feeling . . .

Like a tombstone . . .

Yes. And I have the feeling that 1960 was a year of reconsideration and evaluation, despite all the normal activity . . .

Again, let me use the occasion of these students I've been talking with. Ten years ago everyone was much interested in anthropology and the humanistic sciences. Interested in the question of origins, of how the concept of culture could be extended in that sense. Just now the parallel people, the students now in college, seem very concerned with theories of knowledge, with communications systems—with the autonomic nervous system, for example. With what people like Skinner and Joshua Whatmouth are doing with the statistical analysis of languages and all the problems of control. That's where William Burroughs becomes interesting. *Naked Lunch* is about control, however much it's about other things too. I see what you mean by a sense of conclusion. I don't think it is *a* conclusion. It's one conclusion—men arrive at many conclusions in their lives, in all senses. I think that in 1945, remembering that that's an arbitrary date, a war had ended, and men of my particular generation felt almost an immediate impatience with what was then to be regarded as a solution. Many of us had been involved in this huge global nightmare, and we came back to our specific personal lives, situations, feeling a great confusion and at times a great resentment about what had been given us as a rationale for all this. So we had that reason to move upon something—upon a clarity that could confront these dilemmas more adequately than the generalities we had been given.

We also had, of course, the very specific example of William Carlos Williams, who, in 1945, I don't think was even regarded as a minor poet. It's curious to remember that. Somewhere around 1950-55 I remember reading an article in the *Hudson Review* in which he was dismissed as a "paranoid mumbler." Now the same journal today would not make the same statement. So there's been that change.

I feel almost as though we will not have to go back, but of course we'll now have to qualify ourselves again. The revolution, or at least the "minor renaissance" that Kenneth Rexroth mentioned in the *New York Times,* is this period. I feel I'm just getting started, in other words. I'm not saying this like Sam Smiles, but everytime I look at what I've done, I wonder. I've done it, so now I have something else to do. I can't rest, in that sense. There's no rest for the wicked. Again a New Englandism.

You've mentioned New England several times. You were born in Massachusetts, weren't you?

Yes, in Arlington, just outside of Boston. But I actually grew up in a pretty rural background—on a farm, although it wasn't actually worked as one. It gave me that kind of atmosphere, and gave me that sense of speech as a laconic, ironic, compressed way of saying something to someone. To say as little as possible as often as possible.

You were involved with the beginning of Cid Corman's magazine Origin, *were you not?*

Yes. In fairness to Cid I ought to make very clear that it was his editing and his work that made *Origin* what it subsequently proved. What had happened was simply that I had got in contact with Cid through the radio program he then had, and we weren't satisfied with what we found in available poets. I guess the men we might have looked to were pretty much tied up in other senses. Remember the poetry that comes out of the 30's and 40's is a socially orientated poetry. By that I mean that it is engaged primarily with problems of sociology —either ironic comment upon urbane or urban situations, or else a continuing of a tradition of that kind, say, from Ransom, Tate and such older men. William Jay Smith is an instance, Randall Jarrell partly an instance, and Karl Shapiro very much an instance of this kind of writing. We wanted to bring our terms of writing up to the actual poem we were writing. We didn't want to remember anything. We wanted to have the actual issue of the poem in the poem as we were writing it. So Cid got in touch with Olson and Denise Levertov and Paul Blackburn, and that began it, I think.

What about the Divers Press, which printed many first volumes of poetry?

Well, I think many writers begin by taking on the problem of getting their work printed. I wanted a press that would be of use to specific people, including myself. I printed two of my own books, two of Blackburn's, and I printed Olson, Irving Layton and so on. We had to. We had to have the dignity of our own statement. We had to have it in a form that could be available to other people. So, we were lucky enough to be in a place where there was inexpensive printing to be got, and we were off. I think Jonathan Williams has done a great deal in this same area. I think of recent correspondence with James Purdy. He printed his first books himself, and luckily Edith Sitwell saw a copy. In other words, you cannot get your poems out where they ought to be if you don't do something about it. So we put our books out. God, we were laughed at, but that was part of it too.

W. S. Merwin

Merwin talked with me in January 1961, just after beginning a tour as poetry Editor for *The Nation*. He's the author of several books of poetry (the latest being *The Drunk in the Furnace*) and translation, with more to appear soon. He was the Yale Younger Poet in 1953, but his new poems, he says, "bear little relation to what's in my books."

You have written several plays; is playwriting incidental with you?

I think it's not only incidental, but past. I think I'm working my way out the other side of that. I thought for several years that I was a playwright, but I was probably fooling myself.

You had a Rockefeller Fellowship and a play produced here in 1956 . . .

These things don't make you a playwright. I wrote four plays, each of them quite different from the others and none of them satisfied me. I ended up after the fourth without any great desire to write any more. I think that answers it for the time being anyway.

What was the impulse to write plays in the first place?

Great fascination with the theater, which I no longer have, and a fascination with simply writing plays—with that way of writing—which I don't have any more either. The first play was a verse play, and that made me feel that I didn't want to write any more verse plays, for a number of reasons. I don't feel terribly indentified with those plays, least of all the verse play. I wrote that very young, I don't think it was a very good subject and the development was melodramatic.

What about verse plays in the style of Beckett and Ionesco?

Well, that's something quite different. I mean, if you call that a verse play, that's still interesting. But that's the only kind of playwriting that I'd be remotely interested in.

Your last book was published by Macmillan and the one previous was imported by Knopf. Could you tell me what the feeling on the part of such major book publishers is about the publication of poetry?

This is pure hunch on my part, because whenever something of mine was published, I seem not to have been around. It can't be based on any knowledge of the publishing field, but I've a feeling the publishers are welcoming poetry more than they were fifteen years ago. Why they should be, I don't know; perhaps they've felt that, after all, they may not make much money on poetry, but they aren't going to lose much either—which is a reasonable position.

Five years ago, everybody wanted autobiographies. Every-time you had anything to do with a publisher, he said, "What about writing an autobiography?" and I could never understand this, because publishers are always losing their shirts on autobiographies. They never lose their shirts over a book of poems. I think it's probably that more people are interested in poetry than were interested in it ten years ago.

Why do you think there is a resurgence of interest in poetry?

That's a hell of a big question. I think the penny's dropping, that's why. Or I think that's one reason—the feeling that there's not much time and it can't last the way it is. If a feeling of crisis goes on long enough, I suppose, one of two things happens—either a person or a society becomes numbed or they get interested in poetry. This has happened in practically all the wars you can think of since the time of the Industrial Revolution. The great periods when people were interested in poetry, though not necessarily the great periods for writing it, were times when something critical was, at least, in the wind. Having said this I immediately think of a whole barrage of exceptions.

It seems to me that you, among others, represent a kind of "middle ground" in contemporary poetry—neither "Academic" nor "New American." Would you agree with that?

I suppose so. I don't know what either "school" is supposed to consist of, but I don't think I've ever been a part of either. I don't quite see that that necessarily lands me in the "middle" of anything though. Whatever you want to call it, my position, insofar as I have one, wasn't sort of worked out in advance; I was living a great part of the time away from literary doings, not seeing many other writers or literary people, and it worked out that way. And there's another thing—I had the luck to start publishing when I was really pretty young and it's sometimes just assumed that what I'm doing now or trying to do now must be just about the same as what I was doing as much as ten years ago. Or more.

T. S. Eliot recently caused a stir by saying that poetry should not be taught. What's your reaction to that?

Right. I think it ultimately obscures what the whole thing is about and I've had deliberately little to do with it, because I feel quite strongly that it's not for me. Most of my friends have either taught "creative writing," or had something to do with the teaching of it at some time or another, but I think it's quite wrong for me and so I've never had anything to do with it. The time at which students are being taught these things is when they should be finding out a number of things for themselves, and the worst people to teach them is the older generation—unless they themselves seek out the older generation. Even that's suspicious.

Writing should be a completely unorganized, uninstitutionalized thing; it shouldn't be a matter of generalizations, such as I'm making now. One of the things I think potential writers, particularly poets, should be finding out is the fact that they have to learn to confront their own experience in their own way. And to be told about relations with traditions and with writing and with "making an honest attitude" by somebody older—however wise and however well-meaning and liberal—is pretty dangerous. These things can only be learned by risks—risking learning nothing at all and getting into trouble and making a fool of yourself. I've a rather romantic feeling that if you reach an age somewhere in the twenties without making a big fool of yourself in some way, it's unlikely that you're going to be much of a writer. If too much gentle wisdom and rightness come too early—it's impossible to be right or to be taught to be right at that age.

What you can be taught is that the present is not separate from the tradition, but it's not the same, either. You can be taught that people have been in danger before and the way they behaved, then you can figure out what all that has to do with you. Between the ages of sixteen and twenty, if you aren't finding out any of this yourself, you're going to find it hard to find out for yourself later—you're going to go on taking other people's advice. I suppose that this is far too intimate and too personal a thing to be taught.

One reason that so many writers end up teaching is simply to support themselves and their family. Where else can they go?

This is a problem every poet has to figure out for himself. I think this is a problem for which there shouldn't be an answer. However, I think that the "creative writing" thing is excellent for somebody who isn't going to be a writer. It's a way of teaching him things about writing which he wouldn't otherwise know. He'll know how to read things better—as long as he doesn't become too presumptuous and figure he knows the whole thing better than the people who wrote it. That's another fault of this thing—people come out having had some sort of reading of Melville and figure they know more about *Moby Dick* than Melville himself knew. Nobody who taught them creative writing had any lessons to teach Melville, I don't think.

My experience has been that the first two years of college are spent largely in teaching the student to be a critic . . .

Well, I think that one of the troubles with criticism in America in particular is the same thing that's the matter with a lot of the other writing: the technical end of it has not become so proficient. In the first place, I'm slightly prejudiced against this form of writing—in general, it bores me. The other thing is that the sense of urgency isn't there—the reason for writing it was probably that some joker had to write another paper in order to keep his next year's tenure at you-name-it college. I don't feel that this is a reason for writing anything. I don't want to ever read another dissertation on "The Middle Years of Henry James."

How do you feel now that you're an editor?

I've been an editor for three afternoons now. It's a very sort of strange experience for me—I've never done it before. I feel very keenly that I'm not an editor, not a teacher, because I pick up an occasional poem and I think, "This is very interesting, but on the other hand, isn't that an awful line or word or phrase and if only this bit were cut here." And then what do you do? I'm aware that, insofar as I'm anything I'm more a writer than I am an editor, if I start monkeying with this, I'll be monkeying it toward the way I would do it—and this isn't fair—this is quite dangerous and highly presumptuous on my part, because if there is any virtue in the poem, it's for the writer himself to find it and not for me to tell him.

So what do I do? Instead of saying, "Why don't you cut your poem and do this," in general, I simply send it back and say, "This was very interesting and I hope you'll try again." If you write to all these people and say to fix it "this way" and then send it back again, then you're practically obliged to publish it and it may not be any better than it was in the first place. This would be old hat to anyone who's edited—but I'm just finding these things out. There's a distressing amount of stuff that smells of "creative writing," you know—and an awful lot of poems about poetry and poems about writing poems. I should be more interested in poems on this subject than I am, I suppose.

I think a writer taking up editing as a pinch-hitting job for a short period comes to it with all his prejudices—at least I do—and I'm trying for them not to be operative, though I haven't got anything else to work with. I haven't got a "critical system." I don't think I could swing one.

One can't put The Nation *into the little magazine category. Why does it publish poetry?*

I think they always have published poetry, for one thing. This was a tradition—after all, *The Nation* is a very old periodical. It goes back into the 19th century, and liberal magazines of opinion in the 19th century automatically published poetry. I think such magazines were rather important in American poetry at one time, and I think this is a good thing. I mean, I like the idea of poetry being published in non-literary, ungentlemanly periodicals.

Do you get a lot of submissions?

An awful lot. In ten days there've been three large cardboard boxes filled to the top with papers. I'm amazed there's as much written as there is.

What's your impression of all this? Is it good?

Most of it is not very good—that goes without saying. That's an enormous understatement too, because most of it's just terrible. And it's pretty depressing, because it's depressing to read bad stuff all the time and besides, these are the poets' pigeons—they've brought them up and they're fond of them, and there's absolutely nothing good you can say about most of them.

Why is this?

I don't see how it can be otherwise. I don't see the theory that there are ever going to be hundreds of thousands of people who can write exciting poems, however much "creative writing" they've learned for however many years. The most that can be taught is skill and there's even a limited number of people who can learn any skill in something as devious and strange and odd in the way it works as poetry.

Do you see any uniform characteristic in the bad poetry?

Yes, there's a certain tendency toward great vagueness and diffuseness. A poem in which there may be imbedded a marvelous poem will run three times its length; or you'll get a poem which sort of tails out into imagery which is absolutely so vague and abstract that nothing can either be understood or seen—a sort of cloud. These are the two main characteristics. Another is the great characteristic of a lot of bad writing—you just can't see any connection between that piece of writing and any conceivable kind of experience. That is simply literary writing.

In other words, you would like to see a specific and a specially oriented kind of poetry?

Yes, I would. I don't see that I can change this simply by walking into *The Nation* office and taking up a box of poems. But I think this is one reason I was asked to do it—because

I did have very definite ideas as to what I wanted to do. All that I can do is to try not to let the prejudices be totally subjective and personal, though some of them amount to principles, I suppose. I think that diffuseness, unless there's a very good reason for it, is a bad thing. I think that concision and sharpness and impact and directness and relation to recognizable experience, however peculiar and remote, are good things.

I like to feel that a poem was about something to the writer—that he wasn't just writing the poem beacuse he had a rainy afternoon or that he felt he'd like to have a poem published. I want to be acutely aware of an experience which the poet has been trying to remake or give sense to as directly as possible. I know there are other kinds of poetry, with their own virtues. What I hate is poetry so-called which is just literature. It's always around—I've written some myself; it seems almost everybody has. I'm looking for exceptions. Among other things, for surprise.

Denise Levertov

Although Denise Levertov was born in England, this fact of birth has not affected her position as one the best of the "new American poets." Her six books have been published by various houses, including City Lights, Jargon and New Directions, the last-named having printed her latest two, the most recent of which is *The Jacob's Ladder*. She has also been poetry Editor for *The Nation*.

Can you give me your statement of faith as a poet? Your aesthetic?

First of all, I believe that the gift of being able to write poetry must always be considered *as* a gift. It's a responsibility, whether one considers it given by God or Nature. It's something which the poet must take seriously. His responsibility is not to himself, not to his career, but to poetry itself. Therefore I believe in craftsmanship and care. And, as a craftsman, I feel that every piece of punctuation, every comma and every colon, is a serious matter and must be duly considered. Punctuation is a tool, all the parts of punctuation and of grammar are tools, and one must use them efficiently.

Then you don't believe in some of the current poetry, in which the first draft is left intact, automatically written, including spelling errors?

No, I certainly don't. I do feel that it's indispensable to a poet to have the initial gift, which is given to him, and over which he has no control. He either has it or he doesn't. And

I believe that every poem must arise from a very deep level of the poet, otherwise it's not alive. It's not going to have life. It's not viable. Incidentally, I think that a part of the poet's equipment is the instinct for knowing when to *begin* writing the poem. A poem which is begun to be put on paper, to be crystallized, too soon, is going to be a poem which, if the poet has a sense of responsibility, is going to need an awful lot of revision. This can be avoided by waiting until the moment is ripe. Once he has crystallized, initially, the poem, then comes in the responsibility of his intelligence and his judgment. Total accidents, (not spelling errors, that's just beneath contempt), but sometimes accidents of syntax, for example, could be functioning parts of the poem.

The poet has to look at the poem after he's written the first draft and consider with his knowledge, with his experience and craftsmanship, what needs doing to this poem. It *may* be complete in itself. He has to have antennae that are going to tell him. He has to feel out what he has there.

How do you know, having just written a first draft, that you have a poem which is right and which will work?

Well, when one has just written a first draft one may be elated, and one may wrongly think that it's right as it stands. But, of course, one has to wait and read it over the next day or the next week. Some people work slowly and some people work fast. I work rather fast. Then, I think one's experience tells one. One spends one's whole life writing poems, (I started writing poems when I was a child and I'm sure many other poets did start young), and has years of reading and years of thinking about poetry and years of writing poems to help one. One doesn't really come out of the blue. It's a question of judgment. How does a painter know when his painting is finished? It's a matter of a synthesis of instincts and intelligence. You can't leave the intelligence out. But you can't *start* with the intelligence; if you start with the intelligence, you have nothing whatsoever. You have a dead baby.

You say "you" and "one" much more than you say "I." Is this also a characteristic of your poetry?

It has been pointed out to me recently that I have tended, in the past, to say "one" or "you" or to leave out those words altogether. But I do believe in the use of the "objective correlative," as Eliot called it. I don't believe that poetry is the raw expression of personal emotion. On the other hand, I don't mean to say that it can't be; but I think that a poet has to be skilled and experienced before he begins using "I." He can come to it eventually; and I'm just really beginning to let myself say "I" because I feel that now I can do it without the kind of crudity with which some people who have just begun to write poetry write about their own feelings.

I always feel that what such people should be doing, if they really want to be poets, is writing objectively. Writing about a chair, a tree outside their window. So much more of themselves really would get into the poem, than when the just say "I." The "I-ness" doesn't come across, because it's too crude, very often. For instance, the objective earlier poems of William Carlos Williams (who, in the ripeness of his old age has been saying "I" in a quite different way) say so much more than what they superficially appear to be saying. They're quite objective little descriptions of this and that, and yet, especially when one adds them together, they say a great deal about the man. In a much deeper, more impressive way than if he'd spent the same years describing his emotions. If a writer only describes how he feels, crudely, it's not very interesting. If he writes about the blackness of the sky and the dirtiness of the sidewalk, the experience is transferred, and we feel oppressed by these things, just as he did.

What do you write about?

I believe in writing about what lies under the hand, in a sense. I think that one should never sort of look around for subjects. I don't believe in the contrived, and I don't like to read poetry which seems to me contrived. Keats said "poetry should come as naturally as the leaves to a tree, or not at all," and I don't think he meant that poetry was a question of "warbling native woodnotes wild." I feel that he meant that poetry arises out of *need*, out of really having something to say about something that we—that the poet—that I—have actually felt or experienced. Not necessarily in the visual world—the external world—it can be an inner experience— but it must be something true.

Do you find that more of your poems are about inner experience?

I think that the poems in *Here and Now*, for example, a few years ago, were very much more about things in the outside world. In the last couple of years I've drawn on experiences equally real to me, but perhaps more private— dreams and inner experiences. But I also believe very much in the concrete image. It's almost hypocritical of me to say that I *believe* in it, because it is natural for me to express myself in concrete images, not in abstractions.

Do you think there has been, in effect, a poetry renaissance?

I don't really know if there's a renaissance. There seem to be more readers, perhaps, for poetry. I think there have always been people writing poetry, and I don't think that the best ones are necessarily those that are most in the public eye. There are a lot of good poets in all the alleged "schools" of poetry. There is a good variety. Scattered all over the country there are interesting poets doing good work. I don't know whether this constitutes a renaissance . . .

LeRoi Jones

Jones published only two more issues of *Yugen* after his interview was recorded early in 1960. Since then, he has co-edited *The Floating Bear* and has seen Corinth's publication of his first book of poems, *Preface to a Twenty Volume Suicide Note,* in association with his own Totem Press. Morrow has scheduled his study, *Blues, Black & White America* and Grove will do his *System of Dante's Inferno.* He continues working on prose, plays and on poems for a second collection.

Yours seems to be one of the three or four "clique" magazines around today, in that it publishes a fairly restricted group of so-called "beat," "San Francisco" and New York writers. Why do you publish this group—this "stable" of writers?

Well, it does seem to fall that way. But for a long time Dr. Williams couldn't get into the *Hudson Review,* and several other mature, older poets like Kenneth Patchen were never admitted there or in magazines like the *Partisan Review* or *Sewanee.* If those editors had a literary point of view in excluding their work, then I feel I have as much right, certainly, to base my choice on my literary taste. If it seems like a coterie—well, it turns out to be that way. There are other reasons—but that's the simplest explanation, actually.

The writers that I publish are really not all "beat" or "San Francisco" or "New York." There are various people who could also fit into other groups—for instance, the people who went to Black Mountain College—and others not affiliated with any real group. But they have some kind of affinity with the other so-called groups—their writing fits into a certain kind of broad category.

Many of the same names appear regularly in Yugen, Big Table, Evergreen . . .

It's a little different though. Most of the people that, say, Paul Carroll prints, he wouldn't have printed if it hadn't been for a magazine like *Yugen*. And *Evergreen Review,* to a great extent, has picked up on things that I've done already and that have appeared in magazines like the *Black Mountain Review* and *Neon.* They pick them up. As a matter of fact, in Paul Carroll's case, I know of at least two poets who appear in his magazine only because of various things he saw in *Yugen* and in an essay I wrote. He said he picked up some things in that essay that enabled him to understand or become more sympathetic with certain people's work.

I'd like to have your thoughts on a kind of contemporary writing that could be illustrated by Frank O'Hara's "Personal Poem" in Yugen *6. In it he describes his thoughts before and after having lunch with one "LeRoi." With its highly and specifically personal references it seems to be more an anecdote of interest to future scholars than something partaking of the heightened qualities of a more traditional poetic nature. What is the validity in this kind of writing?*

I didn't especially think that there was any charted-out area in which the poetic sensibility had to function to make a poem. I thought that anything—anything you could grab—was fit material to write a poem on. That's the way I think about it. Anything in your life, anything you know about or see or understand, you could write a poem about if you're moved to do it. I'm certain that if they have to footnote what the House of Seagrams was in his poem, or who the LeRoi, was, that will only be of interest to academicians and people doing Master's theses. Anybody who is concerned with the *poem* will get it on an emotional level—or they won't get it at all. Certainly, if I didn't like it, I wouldn't go through any book to look up those names with the hope that I would feel moved once I knew where the building was or who LeRoi was. I don't think that means anything at all. I don't think that has anything to do with the *poem*, actually. What the poem means, its function, doesn't have to do with those names—that's just part of it. It doesn't seem to me to be the same kind of stupidity that's found when you have to go to Jessie Weston's book to find out what a whole section of "The Wasteland" means. The House of Seagrams is certainly less obscure than certain Celtic rites. And I don't see what makes it any less valid because it's a casual kind of reference or that it comes out of a person's life, rather than, say, from his academic life.

I'd say that if a poem, as a whole poem, works, then it's a good poem . . .

Right . . .

You once wrote that, "MY POETRY is whatever I think I am. I make a poetry with what I feel is useful and can be saved out of all the garbage of our lives." Would you like to develop that a little more fully?

Well, it's part of what you mentioned about "traditional" poetic areas. I believe that the poet—someone with a tempered sensibility—is able, or should be able to take almost any piece of matter, idea, or whatever, and convert it if he can, into something really beautiful. I don't mean "beautiful" the way Bernard Berenson means it—but into something moving, at least.

And I don't think that there are any kind of standard ideas or sentiments or emotions or anything that have to be in a poem. A poem can be made up of anything so long as it is well made. It can be made up out of any feeling. And if I tried to cut anything out of my life—if there was something in my life that I couldn't talk about . . . it seems monstrous that you can tell almost anything about your life except those things that are most intimate or mean the most to you. That seems a severe paradox.

You've mentioned your influences as including Lorca, Creeley and Olson. What from Lorca—a surrealist approach?

Yes, that, but at the time I got hold of Lorca, I was very much influenced by Eliot, and reading Lorca helped to bring me out of my "Eliot Period" and break that shell—not so much *Poet In New York*, which is the more surreal verse, but the early *Gypsy Ballads*—that kind of feeling and exoticism.

What about the Black Mountain people, and Williams?

From Williams, mostly how to write in my own language— how to write the way I *speak* rather than the way I *think* a poem ought to be written—to write just the way it comes to me, in my own speech, utilizing the rhythms of speech rather than any kind of metrical concept. To talk verse. Spoken verse. From Pound, the same concepts that went into the Imagist's poetry—the idea of the image and what an image ought to be. I learned, probably, about verse from Pound—how a poem should be made, what a poem ought to *look* like—some little inkling. And from Williams, I guess, how to get it out in my own language.

Is there a middle ground between natural speech and formal metrics?

Oh, yes. I don't mean that I write poems completely the way I'm talking now, although I'm certain that a great deal of my natural voice rhythm dominates the line. For instance, my breathing—when I have to stop to inhale or exhale— dictates where I have to break the line in most cases. Sometimes I can bring the line out longer to effect—you learn certain tricks, departures from a set method. But mostly it's the *rhythms* of speech that I utilize, trying to get closer to the way I sound *peculiarly*, as opposed to somebody else.

Does your being a Negro influence the speech patterns—or anything else, for that matter, in your writing?

It could hardly help it. There are certain influences on me, as a Negro person, that certainly wouldn't apply to a poet like Allen Ginsberg. I couldn't have written that poem "Kaddish," for instance. And I'm sure he couldn't write certain things that have to deal with, say, Southern Baptist church rhythms. Everything applies—everything in your life. Sociologically, there are different influences, different things that I've seen, that I know, that Allen or no one knows.

I asked that because I don't find in your work the sense of "being a Negro" that occurs, say, in the poetry of Langston Hughes . . .

That may be part of, like they say, his "stance." You have to set up a certain area in which you're going to stand and write your poems, whether you do it consciously or not. There has to be that stance. He is a Negro. It doesn't lessen my feeling of being a Negro—it's just that that's not the way I write poetry. I'm fully conscious all the time that I am an American Negro, because it's part of my life. But I know also that if I want to say, "I see a bus full of people," I don't have to say, "I am a Negro seeing a bus full of people." I would deal with it when it has to do directly with the poem, and not as a kind of broad generalization that doesn't have much to do with a lot of young writers today who are Negroes. (Although I don't know that many.) It's always been a seperate section of writing that wasn't quite up to the level of the other writing. There were certain definite sociological reasons for it before the Civil War or in the early part of the 20th century, or even in the 30's, but it's a new generation now, and people are beset by other kinds of ideas that don't have much to do with sociology, *per se.*

I'm always aware, in anything I say, of the "sociological configuration"—what it *means* sociologically. But it doesn't have anything to do with what I'm writing at the time.

Edward Dorn

This interview, printed here almost completely unrevised, was recorded when Dorn was in New York in February 1961 on a reading tour. Around that time, Totem Press published his first book, *The Newly Fallen*. He has since gone his quiet way to Pocatello, where he writes, and teaches at Idaho State College.

How long were you at Black Mountain College?

Well, I was there twice—the first time in 1950, the second time in 1954. At the end of that year, I think, the school closed. I think I'm rightly associated with the Black Mountain "school," not because of the way I write, but because I was there. I always thought of the place not as a school at all, but as a climate in which people work closely together and talk. The value of it for me certainly was that, because by the time I'd left the University of Illinois, I didn't much want to go to school anyway. But I certainly went there.

Do you think there is any similarity between the writers who are associated with Black Mountain?

No. I think it was a common atmosphere. Unlike other people I've talked to, I've been unable to find any similarity that interested me between the work of Duncan and Olson, and I don't find much similarity between the work of Olson and Pound, either. It seems to me that Olson is doing something I've never read before, except from his hand. Although I find its basis archaic almost (unlike *Patterson*, which is a work put up in reference to Olson's work quite a lot, as well as the *Cantos*), I don't think any previous work so attempts to tap the realities of a region in all its economic and political and human aspects.

I think the value of being at Black Mountain was that very able people and very alive people were there, back and forth and off and on and through it. And that's what made it a very important place to be. I don't see any superstructure that existed there which would relate people and what they subsequently did, although there might be one, and a case could probably be made for it. But I don't think that it's so important. It was literally a place, and it was very arbitrary. North Carolina is a very unlikely place, say, for people who were mostly from New York and New England, with a very few from the midwest and possibly another very few from the West Coast. There was no important logic connected with why it should be there, so it was a very impersonal site in which to have this go on. And in many ways it was a hostile surrounding, which was more subtile than anything else, I think. But it was good—that kind of isolation, and at that time it was good. I think it has to come at a certain time of your life. That sort of isolation would be very distasteful to me now.

But don't you feel rather isolated, living in New Mexico?

Literally, yes. But I don't ever think of it that way. I read newspapers now, and I never used to. I don't mean anything silly by that—what is going on anywhere interests me in a real way. I was almost afraid to even admit that anything was going on, or that it could possibly be of use or importance to me. That's radically different now.

Has the political side of your poetry been of recent origin, then?

I think it would be necessary to answer that in more ways than one. For one thing it's become clear to me now, after writing more steadily in the past five years than before, that

I don't have anything obscure in me to say. What's obscure in me is what I know. And that's what I try to get at. It may seem a waste of time to get at something you know, and only that, but I think that is a limitation I have, and if I can exploit anything, it will be that, as fully as possible.

When we lived in Burllington, Washington, poems like "A Rick of Wood" came out of a direct influence of what I found myself in. Still then, I wasn't able to feel myself in relationship to a larger world than all those very small valleys and rivers that exist there. And still, I think the first sensible thing I did was to try to make it that way, at least, as a beginning. Now, something much later, like the poem about the Trinity site, is essentially the same thing in a way, except that I'm not, I hope, so bound by what's literally in front of me. Although I don't, at any point, think that's bad, if you can go deep enough into it. It interests me much more to make a political statement as hot as I can, and as impersonal as I can, because, I'm not at the point yet where I can believe that it will ever get anybody to start walking from New York to Hanover. But at this point I can't think of anything more important to say, to me. And I want to say it over and over again, with all the ramifications I can make. I think probably I'll also get over a fear of being vulgar and rough about it. I hope so, because I think that might be beautiful too, and it's time for it, it seems to me.

So much contemporary poetry is utterly urban. Yours seems to me almost completely non-urban . . .

Yes. You see, I don't know the city. I don't know it at all, except to visit it, which I like to do—it intrigues me. I love the city very much, I love New York, but I don't know it and I don't really like to write impressions, just to be writing them. (Although, in one sense, everything I write is an impression of what I want to get at in myself.) Impressions seem a waste of time to me. So it is non-urban, in that sense, but also the greatest concentration of everything in America, as I see it, and as Wyndam Lewis sees it in *America and Cosmic*

Man, is in New York. Still, there are an awful lot of people living elsewhere, and they're really in touch too, in a way.

The line seems to be one of the most important structural considerations in your writing. What is it about the shape of the line, and its relation to your own way of speaking?

In the first place, one inevitably talks about measure and line. It, for some odd reason, remains a technical preoccupation without people knowing very much about it. By very many people, I mean even master poets. I frankly know very little about it. I know what meter is, and I know the names of the various meters, and so forth, but the way I write is really in clots of phrase, and that usually comes out to be Idea, in a vague sense. I don't think Ideas come in units. When the individual line ceases to have energy for me, in those terms, I usually break the line there, with certain exceptions.

Anyone who writes poetry gets into certain habits about how they behave with the line, but I don't think about measure and line, in a technical sense, that much. Clots of phrase, really. And not Olson's "breath," because I'm not sure I understand that unit exactly, although I know what he's talking about. I think that, if it were usable, and if a lot of people were capable of using it, it would be more legitimate than all the current ideas about measure. In any case, it's utterly right for Olson. It's a false problem, in a way, but it's not dead yet, and it will be talked about. But I think it will become less important as the content of our speech becomes more important—as what we're saying becomes more vital to all of us.

One of the things being more recognized now and listened to, I hope, is that poets are saying things important for every human being, and not being just poets so much. I guess I sound dogmatic, but I think we have to face, finally, that there has to be some hope for something actionable to come out of all this. More and more people are writing political poetry, and it's not politics they're writing, at all, it's a fantasy of certain things. It doesn't name, the way poetry in the past has named actual names or substituted names that were well known, for actual names. It isn't that kind of thing that I think is possible today, because, frankly, politics is carried on by literal men—so it's a schoolboy's interest. What can you do with what actually happens in Washington? You can read I. F. Stone, who knows more about it than you could know, anyway.

But the fantasy of politics, in terms of poetry, and the images and the ghosts of that kind of thing are very valuable in terms of the writing and getting of poetry further on a footing of meaning for a large mass of people. And I like that. Now, there will always be an arcane poetry, and only poets, probably, will read it. I don't think, even if this happens, that poets become more and more influential, in the best sense possible, and not in any public sense—I don't think it will really intimidate anybody, because it seems to me that the means of communication are so hopeless that they're there before you are—long before you are—with all their machinery. That seems a desperate thing to me, but it isn't hopeless, because what I really want to do is write, and I'll write more and more politically, I'm sure.

For one thing, I don't know a thing about politics, and I think that gives me the greatest right in the world to be a zealot about it. People who congregate in a square in London and make a march on the atomic works are not really concerned with politics either. Everyone knows the machinery of politics goes on far above our heads, and I don't think there's anything we can do about that. There is energy there to be had, to be put in service of mass statement about this torture, the condition of the world, and I think poets are in a very good position to keep insisting—to lead the way with whatever vision they have.

Allen Ginsberg

After Lawrence Ferlinghetti published *Howl and Other Poems* in 1956, Allen Ginsberg became suddenly and explosively the leader of a new movement in American poetry and, with Jack Kerouac, the leader of the "Beat Generation." Five years later, Ferlinghetti published his second book, *Kaddish and Other Poems,* which was followed by Corinth's *Empty Mirror,* a selection of early work. His *Journals* are still rumored as forthcoming.

About 4 o'clock on December 20, 1960, Ginsberg arrived at the studios. He had just come from an afternoon with James T. Farrell and Leonard Lyons and was full of enthusiasm from the encounter, which he discussed immediately after introducing himself. I had some questions in mind, but few of them were brought up during the course of our ninety-minute conversation, which began by getting down to the problem of producing a program suitable for radio. He asked if he could read anything he wanted and I brought up the difficulty we could have with the F. C. C. on the grounds of "good taste." Ginsberg responded:

My problem is that I write poetry which comes into my mind, and if I read it, it's got to be what I write. I can't read anything I don't write. I once did that, and somebody snuck a tape of it. I did it because the lady didn't have a license for her poetry series, so I thought I'd be polite, at least. I didn't want to bug her or get her mad or anything like that. But I got drunk and read "Howl" and put in the word "censored." It was ridiculous acting—a shameful thing.

So then what finally happened was that Evergreen issued that as a record—to my lasting horror.

Just don't read anything we'd have to cut . . .

The next step of our problem is that the only things I can read are things that I've written. And the last things that I've written, as far as I'm concerned, are the most beautiful things that I've written—the most important things that I've written—and so, the things that I'd naturally read, naturally. They're coming out in a book called *Kaddish and Other Poems.*

Do you want to read from those?

Yes, from those. Except the last manuscripts, the last poems in the book, which are this year's. I went to South America and from South America there's a lot of writing—a lot of little notebooks—and these are from notebook writings. There's a long poem: "Notes on Ether"—having taken some ether in Latin America, sitting in my room—I took notes. But that's long, and that isn't as good as what happened later . . .

All I can do for you is what I can do for you—I can't do anything else. What do you want? Read my poems or not? I think they're more interesting than conversation, in the long run. In fact, that's the "political point" that you're worried about. You asked me if I would make "general comments on the general scene"? Well, this is the comment on the general scene. Right—here—now—in—action! So I call for a union of consciousness, and I prophecy a new Messiah! Because everybody is God, and it's time they seized power in the Universe and took over the means of communication and started communicating!

Ginsberg then read his communication, turning in his thick ring-binder to a manuscript of "Magic Psalm," later included in Kaddish. *After the reading, he said:*

The point of that poem was that there was an abstract divinity outside me that I was trying to summon to my aid or energy. The problem was to integrate it into my own consciousness and to therefore become God, or to say I am God, or to say in the poem "I am God," or to imagine I am God—rather than that God be something external to me. So this is sort of an attempt at the integration—a notation of it.

With that, he read "The End" from Kaddish. *Searching in the binder for other material, he came across a 1959 letter from Gregory Corso, concerning a "vision of death," which lead to Corso's writing "Birthday's End." This brought us to a discussion of exotic drugs, which was momentarily interrupted by my asking why he hadn't published a book since* Howl:

Well, because I didn't think I had anything that was as beautiful and strong enough yet. And then, I left out about three year's work—'55 to '58—though there's some good work in that. That's a separate book that I'll publish, maybe, sooner or later—or wait until I get a Collected Poems. I don't know—it's too much trouble to type all that up and then to send it out. And then, I also felt proud about *Howl,* and wanted to do something finer. Vanity, vanity!

He had recently returned from a writers' conference in Chile which had been responsible for a visit to Brazil and experimentation with local drugs. I asked him who attended the conference:

Ferlinghetti was there from here. And then a whole bunch of people from all over. A bunch of left-wingers and a bunch of Communists and a bunch of anarchists and a bunch of poets and a bunch of young ladies and a bunch of professors, wierdoes, comers . . .

What was in the air?

Confusion. The trouble was that none of them were really interested in writing. They were more interested in politics or sociology or their reputations or being sincere—I don't know what they were interested in. They weren't interested in writing very much. There weren't very many writers there —they were mostly party hacks from South America. By "party hacks" I don't mean the Communist Party—what I mean is hack writers from South America. The party being "reality," or some sense of reality, or some idea that they knew what reality was.

After a brief mention of his encounter with Fidel Castro some days earlier, during Castro's visit to New York, Ginsberg returned to the subject of drugs and drug legislation in the United States. He was particularly adamant on the subject of legalizing marijuana. I asked what else he would legalize:

Well, being an anarchist, I suppose I would legalize everything. I would legalize junk—opiates—to this extent: that junkies should be allowed to go to a doctor and be treated. Because it's a medical problem, it's not a criminal problem. Everybody's treating it like a moral, criminal problem. It's like not treating alcoholics. It's a terrible thing, it's a sadistic thing, it's an awful thing. Everybody knows there's a system in England which has cut it down. The American system of penalizing it has simply driven it underground and created a big black market and therefor made it profitable. They've made it a huge industry—just like Prohibition.

He concluded his discussion of drugs by saying that the only things to which he was "addicted" were ordinary cigarettes. I asked if he were addicted to "joy":

Joy? No, I wish I were addicted to joy. I'm addicted to worry—I'm a worry-wart.

Why? Your poems seem so expansive . . .

Yes, but do you realize how much anxiety I have to go through to get that expansion? I have to see Death, and think I'm seeng Death, and scare myself to Death. To play with my shadow in the mirror. It's terrible.

Do you go from a period of high exaltation with one poem to worrying until you get the next poem?

Well, it's not a poem—it's the exaltation. Usually a poem comes out of it. Exaltation's a corny word—but a nice one. Why not be enthusiastic? Why not be unspeakably enthusiastic?

We talked a little bit about his then current interest in an aspect of Buddhism and I brought up his activities in a film called "Pull My Daisy!"

I didn't think much of the movie as a movie. I thought it was relatively sweet—innocuous. But I thought Kerouac's narration did a great deal—integrated it—made it beautiful—gave it a point that it might not otherwise have had.

Ginsberg then continued by reading selections from his Peruvian journals, written under the influence of ether and other drugs. I asked him about the use of ether:

Ether is a classical Epiphany, did you know about that? And laughing gas was used by Coleridge quite a bit, under the auspices of a guy named Sir Humphrey Davy, who had a house in the Lake Country, and the Lake Poets came to visit and to sniff laughing gas—nitrous oxide. William James recorded various versions of the experience in *The Varieties of Religious Experience,* under the title "The Anesthetic Revelation," so there's a considerable classical stand, you see. Other people used it too. There are all sorts of funny notices of ether in some French Surrealist writing.

Every time I go to my cousin—he's a dentist—he gives it

to me for working on my teeth. Then I wake up and write whatever I can about it. Sometimes it's very funny. Sometimes they're incomprehensible—like the last thing I wrote: "Stick your finger up your knows and you'll know what I mean by one Cosmos." That's very good, I think. I'd put that in a poem, if I had a poem to put it in. I keep getting very strange images under it. Sometimes visual images come through, but very little can I remember. It's a problem, this ungraspable thing—because as your mind disappears, you get to know what's beyond the mind. But then—how can you record it in the mind? I think that we are now coming to a point of a kind of unification of Cosmos—and consciousness—or something. I don't know—something big is happening consciously to consciousness. Everybody's getting hip.

Things seem quiet right now . . .

Right this minute, yes—the interregnum. Well, it's sort of like a question—will the people accept the new consciousness or vomit it up in an atom bomb? But it doesn't make any difference what the answer is, because nothing can be destroyed, really. What was there is always there, so that's all right, I suppose. But that's why I think marijuana is a political tool. It's a catalytic stimulus to a slightly expanded consciousness. Or, as the man from Havana says: "You can't have an army when you're high!" So civilization's got to alter, I suppose, and consciousness. All the realities have got to alter—and they're the dinosaurs who don't want to alter! Poor dinosaurs. I'd put my money on something interesting happening—I put my poetry on it, so to speak—I put my life for it, I think. I guess it'll be the same old thing, happening again. And what is the same old thing? We are all one—man is one—man is brothers—or "Amor Vincet Omnes" was what I thought the other day—"Love Conquers All," through all the universes.

Do you think a poet can ever accomplish anything toward this?

Christ did—for what he accomplished. Buddha did. Whitman did—or he certainly set something going in public consciousness—a sign to people that certainly wakes people up. Blake did.

I was talking with a guy last night—a very beautiful magician I know—speaking of the problems of the subjective worlds and the objective worlds and all that. Are they really different, and how do you ever unify them? It's a question of our taking the deepest of the subjective world and planting it out on the objective world. And not being afraid of death or madness—it's not that dangerous. There's a thing in Apollinaire: "Now is the time for prophecy without death as a consequence." But people are notoriously afraid of subjective experience. The anxiety of it is one thing—the sense of change —but it's not that bad a process. It's just—the only thing to fear is fear itself, I presume.

Do you think the poets are leading this?

No, I think people are leading it. I don't know whether poets lead it—it would be lovely if they did. Poets should lead it. Poets should be the "legislators of the world" as Shelley said. Everybody should lead it.

From this, we turned to a discussion of civil disobedience and the "controls" that governmental agencies place upon action. Ginsberg called investigators "the mind searchers," and their activities "the unconscious psychic plague octopus." He proposed a "truth hour" for radio and television, where anyone could do anything he might want to do. Going back to the ring-binder full of papers, he read a letter from William Burroughs and then discussed the reaction (favorable) of a group of psychiatrists to his reading of his poetry at a symposium on "The Beat Generation." I suggested that some of his remarks resembled those of some members of the Dada movement:

That's true. The Dadaists are very interesting. There's a

lot of Dada rebirth, revival now, because they did develop some interesting techniques. But the impression I get is that consciousness has moved on, so that what they were dealing with then was a 19th century, more humanistic attempt to shake a baby rattle and then make sense on humane, mature terms. They thought that if they let out their aggressions, people would listen, maybe, and they could talk like human beings. But I don't think they were dealing with the problems of visionary consciousness—I think that's what they intuited and what they were working toward, and possibly the great Dadaists were working within . . .

But now everybody's having visions! That's what it boils down to. Really, truely having visions. And now there are these new "wisdom drugs"—lysergic acid, mescalin. Many, many people have taken peyote now—thousands and thousands—and it's legal. And it's freedom of religion. It's inescapable—people are beginning to see that the Kingdom of Heaven is within them, instead of thinking it's outside, up in the sky and that it can't be here on earth. It's time to seize power in the Universe, that's what I say—that's my "political statement." Time to seize power over the entire Universe. Not merely over Russia or America—seize power over the moon—take the sun over.

Ginsberg's last comment called to mind a poem he had written (also in Kaddish), *called "POEM Rocket." To his reading of this, he added a new phrase which he had just thought of: "sunflower monkeys of Uranus." He then read Corso's "Birthday's End," after which I remarked on the 18th century feeling I got from Corso's writing:*

Yes—Shelleyan. His god is Shelley—he taught me Shelley.

As we adjourned, Ginsberg made a final, revealing comment:

I was high on T—I got high at Farrell's house before I came over. I think that was responsible for my being so relaxed and assertive. Usually, I have this problem—it's too difficult—I get nervous—I feel I shouldn't talk about this or that obsession . . .

He was, by this time, completely "sober," and wrote me some days later that "it was the situation, not what was said, that gave what was said some significance." I believe, however, that much of the hour and a half was indeed significant— at least in revealing some previously half-hidden attitudes about his creative process.